T0353809

2016 Election and Beyond
What Did You Know? What You Need to Know

Educator's Perspective

Authors
Joanne Bosley- Wisdom, EdS, and
Dr. Doris McNeil-Sutton, PhD.

iUniverse books may be ordered through booksellers or by contacting:

iUniverse
1663 Liberty Drive
Bloomington, IN 47403
www.iuniverse.com
1-800-Authors (1-800-288-4677)

Because of the dynamic nature of the Internet, any web addresses or links contained in this book may have changed since publication and may no longer be valid. The views expressed in this work are solely those of the author and do not necessarily reflect the views of the publisher, and the publisher hereby disclaims any responsibility for them.

Any people depicted in stock imagery provided by Thinkstock are models, and such images are being used for illustrative purposes only. Certain stock imagery © Thinkstock.

ISBN: 978-1-5320-3968-3 (sc)
ISBN: 978-1-5320-3969-0 (e)

Library of Congress Control Number: 2017919332

Print information available on the last page.

iUniverse rev. date: 01/22/2018

Contents

Preface

"The Sleeping Giant in America is the American People"

As educators, with a combination of 64 years of teaching and learning experience, we wanted to examine the cause and effects of the 2016 election. We decided to write this book because it was evident throughout the election that many people we came in contact with seemingly were ambiguous or unknowledgeable about terms and concepts discussed during the campaign. Some of the questions we considered were threefold. First, were people thinking critically about the rhetorical language and tone of the 2016 presidential campaign? Second, was divisiveness and misinformation becoming a catalyst for election results? Third, we also pondered why some individuals seemed to lack knowledge of various political ideologies presented throughout the campaign. As educators we believe rhetorical language during rallies used to mobilize supporters would negatively affect future generations of young people who aspire to be socially and politically conscious. As scholars, we wanted to examine what would be the long-term consequences of the utilization of undocumented information being referred to as "alternative facts."

We discussed the role of prominent individuals in the campaign, historical events, campaign promises made and situations that influenced the outcome of the election. A summary and analysis of Senator Clinton and Mr. Trump's presidential campaigns was examined. We also explored the accomplishments or lack of achievements during the first 100 days of Trump's presidency.

Another consideration for writing the book was to examine the unforeseen power of "Reality TV" and how millions of Americans seemingly were immune to overt dramatization of unprofessional behavior exhibited throughout the campaign. Additionally, we examined why people, who use technology on a daily basis did not realize the impact social media would have on a 21st-century campaign. Twitter, Instagram, Facebook and e-mails became the unforeseen technology in the election that compelled Mr. Trump to victory.

As educators, we hoped to enlighten individuals who were perplexed as to how and why Mr. Trump won the election when Senator Clinton won three million or more popular votes. Do people have an understanding of how the democratic voting and Electoral College systems could impact the entire election process?

It is our obligation as educators to address civil rights, freedom of speech, and American citizens' rights to protest as outlined in the 1st Amendment of the Constitution. Therefore, we felt obligated to highlight specific sections of the United States Constitution as it pertains to the Electoral process with the hope of educating adults and students throughout America.

This book will also help to generate dialogue on why terms such as fascism and nationalism were mentioned during the campaigns. We found it necessary to address why some Americans felt blindsided when it came to hidden racism, sexism, anti-Semitism and homophobia that still exists in America. Our hope is to facilitate inquiry and dialog about the economic systems throughout the world, and how it could impact people lives on a daily basis. As educational agents for social change, we felt it was not only important to write a book that would generate discussion but also to promote an understanding of why certain events transpired during the 2016 election. We firmly believe this book will be a unique resource for educators, students, and all American citizens because "Knowledge is Power".

Introduction

"The role of educators for social change is to render information and knowledge that enable people to make positive academic, social and political decisions."

The campaign of 2016 was an eye-opener for many people in America. It was as though, "while Americans were sleeping," a new era of history was about to become a reality for America. What was amazing was the way the campaign was organized and conducted. It seemed to be more like a reality show than a real election. There was name calling by both campaigns of Senator Clinton and Donald Trump. Most depressing was Mr. Trumps' insensitivity and imitation of a New York Times reporter with a disability during one of his campaign stops. It was also unreal to see a professional businessman use profanity throughout the campaign. Nevertheless, Donald Trump won the election. One had to question why Trump supporters overlooked this behavior. Is it possible none of his supporters were sympathetic to someone who has a disability? Was racism, economic interest, nationalism or the "desire to clean the swamp" (which meant to get the old guards or the establishment out of the White House) the overwhelming surge that influenced their support?

This book covers both campaigns and what worked and what didn't. We identified the historical relationships between the past and present, political figures, class structures and the art of politics. A comprehensive discussion of political terminology, campaign strategies, political ideologies, historical events, and various economic systems were discussed throughout the book. Statistical data regarding poverty and what causes poverty in the United States including the opioid epidemic was explored. No book about the 2016 election is complete without a look at President Obama campaign platform for 2008 and 2012 and Senator Sanders' impact on the election of 2016.

We examined past behavior of a dictator and how Trump came to power. It was interesting to note that Mr. Trump supporters could not comprehend that Donald Trump is a member of an establishment (The Billionaire Club).

What was also alarming was Mr. Trumps' anti-establishment rhetoric although he technically wasn't a member of the political establishment but often desired to be part of it.

Clinton email controversy was at the forefront of the campaign. Too much time was delegated to the hacking of Senator Clinton and DNC servers as well as the leaking of e-mails by Wiki Leaks. When Senator Clintons' email server was investigated by the Director of the FBI (Federal Bureau of Investigation) Mr. James Comey, it was determined that no criminal acts had been committed, and only carelessness in preserving government information had taken place. Mr. Trump used the hearings and investigation as a calling card to justify the slogan, "Lock her up!" over and over again at his rallies. Furthermore, the aspect of the campaign that was most disturbing and painful to watch was the inappropriate sexual behaviors as was evidenced in a nationally televised "Access Hollywood " video with Trump and Billy Bush (radio and television personality) wherein Mr. Trump is seen discussing women private body parts. His subsequent comments supported the notion that it was okay to physically violate females because he was a successful businessman and a TV star. Throughout the campaign, a misrepresentation of the facts fell on both candidates' shoulders. However, several reports indicated that Donald Trump misrepresented facts more often than Senator Clinton. Although, the rhetoric used may have amused some Americans, others were frustrated. The logical step was to examine how and why this type of political campaign manifested itself in 21st century America.

Struggle for Political Power in 2016

"The definition of the term Politics, by Webster Dictionary is the activities, actions, and policies that are used to gain and hold power in a government or to influence a government. Also, one can say, that politics is someone's opinions how to manage the affairs of the local, state, or federal, government".

Politics can be seen as the art of persuasion, which means convincing other to support a position, particular issue, situation the politicians believe in. An aspect of politics includes the fact that some politicians historically, tends to embellish the truth and some even lie. In the case of local, state, federal campaigns, politics can manifest itself as a spider web of contradictions, deceit, misinformation, deception, misrepresentation of facts (*Alternate Facts*) and division.

Politicians use pollsters to poll people to discover what political issues are at the forefront of American minds. Politicians and their organizers read the data/information collected from polls. They use this information to rally their base as well as build upon the data to increase or accumulate more supporters. Even though, some folks say, they don't believe in politics; these same individuals interface with politics every day of their lives. It can be at their job, relationships with others, and their place of worship. Therefore, it's important to understand the impact politics have on our lives and especially the impact of the 2016 election.

Pollsters Impact on the 2016 Campaign

"Did They Get it Wrong in 2016"?

How do pollsters collect their data? Well, there are many ways to collect statistical data.

One must also remember that throughout every political campaign; many candidates rely on pollsters to keep them and the public abreast of how each candidate is doing throughout an election. In 2016 it seemed the pollsters got it wrong. How do pollster collect their data, well there are many types of collection methods. Some use probability sample, which includes random-digit dialing

(RDD). This approach includes sample telephone area codes.

They add random digits to the end to generate 10-digit phone numbers. The practice is the standard practiced by many pollsters. The advantage of this system is that it covers a large population of citizens. This method may generate non-working numbers and is usually very costly.

Another method for collecting data is the Household Sample Selection, wherein in a household in which more than one eligible voter resides, based on election polls, more than one registered voter; this is helpful in producing a random sample of the electorate. The problem becomes that when someone answers the telephone, the response may not necessarily result in a representative sample.

Registration-Based Sampling (RBS), is the sampling of individuals drawn from a registered voters list. These voters' telephone numbers matched to a voter registration list. One of the best ways to collect data because it is inexpensive and more efficient because, most of the time, the pollster can reach a working phone number. The problem that exists with this type of polling is voters registration list do not include unlisted telephone numbers.

A Pollster also may use a non-probability sample. Wherein, voters access what is called a dial-in-polls, which is popular with media outlets and internet polling sites. However, these self- selected surveys based systems, are not always reliable. Regardless, of what system pollsters used in 2016, the individuals who either mislead the pollster for whatever reason or toward the end of the campaign decided to vote opposite of what the told the pollster.

Politics and Race Relationships in 2016

If polls, many Americans will say that race play no significant role in how they voted in 2016, and many of these voters may be telling the truth. However, did you know politicians do not have to utilize outward racial statements they can make dog whistle statements that can be heard by their supporters? Politicians can also use idioms consisting of mode of expressions/phrases and images that audience understand. Furthermore, this doesn't mean the politician is racist. However, one must remember the primary objective of any politician is to win.

Politics and Historical Relationships

"Did Nationalistic Rhetoric Opened the Gates of Hell and Racism Escaped"?

Adolph Hitler

Most people know who Adolph is, however, do not understand how Adolph became the leader of the Third Reich. Adolf Hitler' started his rise to power in Germany in September 1919 by joining the Germany Workers Party and went on to become the

National Socialist German Workers leader in 1920. This political party referred to as the Nazi Party believed in extreme nationalism, Pan-Germanism, and anti-Semitism. Hitler's inner circle believed in loyalty and devotion to Germany. Also, his followers possess a sense of national consciousness and believe in exalting their nation above all others. Adolph's place his primary emphasis on propping up Germany.

Hitler never used the slogan of "Let Make Germany Great Again" however he did recruit Josef Goebbels in 1929 to be his Minister of Propaganda. Goebbels developed a successful campaign by using simple slogans and images repeated over and again. This strategy was successful in winning support from the party. Lots of money was spent on newspapers, leaflet, and poster for the campaign. Goebbels' plan for controlling the mass media was the instrument that helped established a cult of personality around Hitler. Rallies and speeches were broadcast on radio, cheaply, because the state produced them.

Why the discussion of Adolph Hitler? Sometimes it's essential to connect the dots from the past to the present and understand how someone's political rhetoric and policies, can unknowingly excite elements of dangerous behavior that impact millions of people lives. In the case of Chancellor Adolf Hitler, referred to as the Fuhrer, or "Leader" used rhetoric and Nazi- nationalism dogmas as a catalyst that caused millions of Jewish citizens to die or exported and exterminated at Nazi's concentrations camps. We also must not forget there, were other victims of Nazi crimes such as ethnic Poles, Slavs, and Soviet POWs, who were either placed in concentration camps or brutally murdered. Also, it is important to remember, that close to the end of Adolph Hitler, the German people started to realize their "Fuhrer, was a pathological liar, narcissists, and a drug attics. That is why during election campaigns citizens should not only listen to the candidate. But also think critically about the candidate promises, political rhetoric, and policies. Why, because sometimes, history does repeat itself.

Candidate Trump:

What possessed Mr. Trump to use the Nazi salute at one of his campaign rallies? Did he realize that Adolph Hitler and the KKK used this salute to demonstrate patriotism to the nationalist movement? Did Trump utilize jesters to mobilize the nationalists who supported his campaign efforts? Or was he unaware that some of his supporters could be Jewish, Polish or African Americans? Was Donald Trump mindful of the fact that this salute was a painful reminder of what happened to Jewish and Polish citizens in Europe and African-American in the United States? This arm raised salute was and still is utilized by the KKK in America, as well as during the KKK lynching of African-Americans in the

South. What could possess anyone in the 21st century to use such a symbol or jesters that brought so much pain to millions of people? Even though candidate Trump, who became President Trump, claims he disavowed the nationalist, fascist and Alt-Right movement, some of the same individuals helped put him in office in January 2017, and quiet as it is kept, some of these same people still support Mr. Trump.

Did Mr. Trump realize that his campaign promise of deportation of Mexican immigrates would turn a broken immigration system into a humanitarian disaster or did Trump care? One would like to think he didn't understand. It was in America's best interest to fix broken components of the immigration system rather than deport immigrants who worked hard and created no legal problems in America. Did President Trump know the deportation policies would cause many Americans to relate his deportation policy to what took place in Germany (under Hitler's regime) in September 1941? Did Mr. Trump realize there would be fallout from his Muslim ban and it would be viewed as religious discrimination? The deportation rhetoric generated over 867 reported acts of verbal and physical harassment recorded by the Southern Poverty Law Center. Unfortunately, there were numerous anti-Semitic incidents of vandalism and damage to Jewish cemeteries as well as 65% or more anti-Muslims hate crimes across America.

https://www.splcenter.org

"Words do Matter"

There were almost 900 reported 'hate incidents' across the country in the days immediately following Donald Trump's becoming President of the United States. A total of 867 alleged incidents took place across the country, with some being recorded in all but three states - Hawaii, North Dakota, and South Dakota.

California led the way with 99 incidents, before New York and Texas rounded out the top-three with 69 and 57 respectively. This report, which was researched and published by the Southern Poverty Law Center, specifically pointed to Trump in its introduction.

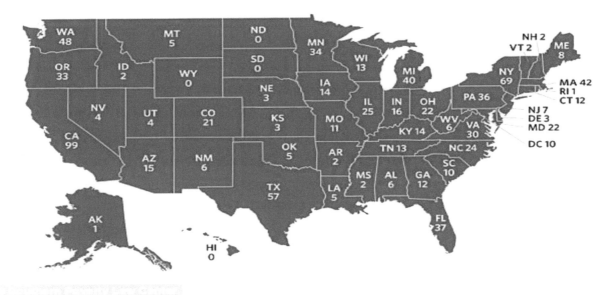

867 POST-ELECTION HATE INCIDENTS

This map shows where all the reported 'hate incidents' took place across the country in the 10 days following Donald Trump's election win https://www.splcenter.org

Post-Election Hate Crimes in Charlottesville, Virginia

"Is Nationalism on the Rise in America?"

White Nationalist March with Torches in Charlottesville, Virginia

Some Americans believe nationalistic hate mongering has been drummed down. Americans felt this way because some young Americans had not seen nationalists' protest like the one witnessed on August 11, 2017. KKK, Alt-Right, and Nazis seem to have quietly built their membership based and came together for a "Unite the Right" rally in Charlottes Virginia at "University of Virginia" campus. They were carrying torches and protesting the removal of General Robert E. Lee statue. During the march, they shouted racist slogans that generated outrage from politicians, Virginia residents and anti-nationalist protesters. It must be noted that the alt-right protesters did have a permit to March.

The slogans shouted were offensive and hurtful to many Americans. The slogans included, "blood and soil," "white lives matter," "you will not replace us," and "unite the right." One slogan that was incredibly hurtful and outrageous was "blood and soul" which brought back painful memories for thousands of Jewish Americans. The "Blut and Boden" slogan espoused was part of the Nazi philosophy, created and used by Richard Walter Darre, the Nazis' minister of agriculture in 1933 and 1942 Germany. The other component and bad memories associated with the Unite the Right Protest was the fact that General Lee was a slave owner and forth to preserve slavery. However, counter-protesters and University of Virginia students were outraged and came out to protest the nationalist marching around their campus.

KKK, Neo-Nazi, and Nationalists, were able to use the same permit on August 12, during a marched and rally in downtown Charlottesville. The "Unite the Right protesters" wore the typical Ku Klux Klan and the Nazi apparel. David Duke and Richard Spencer were leading spoke people for the alt-right movement, were front and center. Counter-protesters were out in force, chanting progressive slogans, and singing civil rights songs. The Charlottesville Police saw the downtown protest as an unlawful gathering and tried to disburse both groups. Nevertheless, both sides continued to March throughout Charlottesville.

The most devastating and sad components of the protest was when a female civil right activist was killed, an African-American male was brutally beaten in a public parking garage by nationalists and 19 others were injured.

Also, to make Nationalists rallies even more egregious was the death of two state police officers when their helicopter crashed while patrolling the demonstrations.

Known White Supremacists

Several white supremacists were at the rallies on August 11, 2017. The most prominent ones were front and center and listed below.

•David Duke the former grand wizard Ku Klux Klan (KKK) which is the oldest right supremacist hate group in America. Even though African Americans are typically the Klan's primary target, they also attack Jews, immigrants, gays, and lesbians and until recently, Catholics.

•Richard Spencer is a white nationalist who believes that white people are superior to people of other nationalities. Hate groups have roots in scientific racism and rely on pseudoscientific arguments, which are absent from scientific evidence. Like neo-Nazism, white supremacists typically oppose people of color, as well as people of most religions.

•Christopher Cantwell is a white supremacist who hates African-American, Jews and anyone with a religious belief he doesn't support.

Who is the Alt-Left Group Antifa?

The term Antifa is short for anti-fascists. They do not adhere to Democratic Party policies. Their political beliefs lean toward the left -- often the far left. The group does not have leadership or headquarters. They hold regular meetings in different states.

•Members of Antifa support oppressed populations and protest the amassing of wealth by corporations and elites. Unfortunately, some of the members employ radical or militant tactics to get their message across.

History of Antifa

Antifa origin is unspecified. However, their beginning is traced back to Nazi Germany and the Anti-Fascist Movement. This militant group was founded in the 1980s in the United Kingdom. Today's members have become more active in making themselves known at community rallies. They are trying to get recognition by inciting violence at Alt-right political gatherings, through small group meetings and social networking.

The President Speaks out on the Charlottesville, Virginia's Rally

"Nationalism is an infantile disease. It is the measles of mankind".
By Albert Einstein

The President spoke about the racist rally in Charlottesville, Virginia on August 11. 2017. His comments seemed to suggest that both parties involved were responsible for the violence that broke out. People watching the newscast, correctly wondered what just happened? However, it was good that the President spoke about the rally in Charlottesville, Virginia on August 11, 2017. Unfortunately, his comments seem to suggest both parties involved were responsible for the violence and was insulting to many members of congress both Democrats, and Republicans. What has become common knowledge is our Commander-in-Chief cannot tolerate criticism, so on August 12, 2017, the President decided to change his statements. Regrettably, he still did not call out the white nationalists or the alt-right. The President felt it was necessary to render a historical analysis of the racism in Charlottesville, Virginia. He repeated that both sides were responsible and racism has persisted in America for a long time. Using his trademark hyperbole as a way of speaking, he doubles down on his statements by repeating it a second time. The President did, however, offered his condolences to the family of the woman killed, two Virginia state toppers who died when their helicopter crashed while monitoring the rally and individuals who were injured.

"As he thinks, so he is; as he continues to think, so he remains." "A man is literally what he thinks, his character being the complete sum of all his thoughts." "A person is limited only by the thoughts that he chooses."
By James Allen

August 14, 2017, the President retracted his previously statements of August 12, in a combative exchange with reporters at Trump Tower in Manhattan.

"President Trump Inability to call a Spade a Spade"

President Trump's August 12, 2017, Statements Regarding the Charlottesville, VA Alt-Right Rally Caused Political Fallout.

"What a sad era when it is easier to smash an atom than a prejudice."
By, Albert Einstein

The President statements of August 12, 2017 forced many politicians to speak out. Democrats and Republicans called the President out on his language and failure to denounce the organizers of the "Unite the Right" rally. Did the President sincerely understand the pain and suffering the Alt-Right Nationalists may have caused for millions of Americans during slavery and throughout the rise of Nazism in Germany?

Chaos in the White House

"What a *tangled web we weave when at first we practice to deceive*"
By Walter Scott

Did you know some top executives quit President's Trump's business and manufacturing advisory councils directly or indirectly? Some of the executives were discouraged about the President's remarks regarding the violence that took place in Charlottesville, Virginia, in August of 2017. What was the President thinking when he commented that there was violence on both sides. It probably didn't matter to the President because the manufacturing advisory committee has not set forth a definite agenda for 2017.

The business and manufacturing advisory councils was an asset to the President promise to create jobs for the unemployed and disenfranchised. Listed below are the members who resigned from the President's business and manufacturing advisory council.

- **CEO OF MERCK & CO.**, Kenneth Frazier
- **CEO OF UNDER ARMOUR**, Kevin Plank
- **CEO OF INTEL**, Brian Krzanich
- **PRESIDENT OF THE ALLIANCE FOR AMERICAN MANUFACTURING,** Scott Paul
- **AFL-CIO**, Richard Trumks, President and Thea Lee, Deputy Chief Of Staff
- **CEO OF 3M**, Inge Thulin
- **CEO OF CAMPBELL SOUP**, Denise Morrison
- **CHAIRMAN OF GENERAL ELECTRIC,** Jeff Immelt

President Trump eventually dismantled his economic advisory and manufacturing councils

President Trump Controversies

"Drama, Drama and More Drama"

- Fires Reince Priebus
- Hires John Kelly
- Hires "The Mooch"
- Fires "The Mooch"
- Fires "FBI Director James B. Comey"
- Publicly Shames Speaker of the Senate AG Sessions

- "Repeal and replace" *Obama Care* did not passed.
- Shames Republicans who voted against Obama Care
- Tweets transgender military ban
- Gets political in Boy Scout speech
- Makes up Boy Scout leader call
- Makes up Mexican President call
- Thanks Putin for expelling Americans
- Begrudgingly signs Russia sanctions, then blasts Congress for it
- Condemns, then endorses anonymous White House leaks
- Encourages cops to rough up suspects
- Publicly shames Mitch McConnell
- Embraces unpassable immigration plan
- Threatens North Korea with nuke
- Bannon says no to military option
- Threatens Venezuela
- Blames "both sides" in Charlottesville
- Shames CEOs who ditch business councils
- Two business councils disband
- Retweets right-wing conspiracy theorist
- Sheriff Apria pardon
- Promotes his Charlottesville winery
- Constantly Tweeting and making negative comments about formers presidents, especially ex-President Obama
- World leaders
- Allies
- President Trump problems with some of staff members
- The Pope

- Chief of staff John Kelly was forced to navigate between the President and Secretary of State Rex Tillerson, because Tillerson called President Trump a Moron.

One of the most important jobs of any President is focusing on bringing Americans together. It seems that the President tends to create some of the most outrageous situations. Many Americans who look forward to the daily news reports are burnout from all the negativity pouring out from the Whitehouse. President Trumps' own party, the Republicans, had to pass legislation to stop him from lifting sanctions on Russia. They were appalled at his impulsive decision to ban transgender Americans from the military. Many Republicans and Democrats made it clear that under no terms should he think about firing the attorney general or the special counsel. Republican and Democratic lawmakers have openly defied the President because of growing frustration on Capitol Hill. Many lawmakers are fed up with his unprofessional tweets, his erratic behavior and his inability to conform to pre-existing governing norms. However, many Republicans and some Democrats were still willing to help push through some of his legislation.

President Trump Management Style

"What You See is What You Get?"

Who is the real Donald Trump? To understand the Reality Show Businessman, one must know how he rose to prominence. Donald Trump's real estate career started when young Donald inherited the day-to-day operations of his father's real estate business. He was fortunate in many real estate ventures in Manhattan and New York City. Furthermore, he gained his notability as the host of "The Apprentice", a television game show which ran for fourteen seasons. The show depicted contenders from around the country who wanted to be successful business men and women with various business backgrounds to participate in an "elimination-style" competition. The show averaged 6.3 million viewers weekly. The punchline, "You're Fired," gave the show its notoriety.

Did you know that President Trump graduated from one of the most prestigious colleges in America? Yes, the University of Pennsylvania-Wharton School of Finance, with a Bachelor of Science degree? He is well educated and more than likely, an intelligent individual. Why is this important? It is important because it may shine a light on the Presidents' leadership style? If the President had to take economic courses at Wharton, he probably studied business management styles and economics. If this is the case, you may want to consider the characteristics listed below.

All Leadership Styles Are Not the Same

For example, (1) Autocratic leadership style: known as authoritarian leadership. Type of leadership wherein one individual controls all decisions and encourages little input from others. The autocratic manager typically makes choices based on ideas and judgments. They rarely accept advice from others. (2) Persuasive leadership style may share some characteristics with an autocratic leader. An essential aspect of the Persuasive leader is to retain control over the whole decision-making process. (3) The Democratic leader encourages other members to take part in the decision-making process-- therefore everything is agreed upon by the majority. (4) Chaotic leadership style gives others the power to make all of their own decisions.

(5) Laissez-faire leadership style is the direct opposite of autocratic management.

Instead of a single leader making all decisions for an organization, Laissez-faire leaders make few decisions and allow others to choose appropriate solutions to a situation.

If you have been following the Commander-In-Chief (President Trump) management or leadership style read below:

(1) When things are going well our President is all photo-op and smiles.

(2) Sometimes the Commander-in-Chief exhibits duplicitous behavior and has been called out for his deceitful (lying).

(3) Sometimes he seems cunning (a crafty use of trickery)

(4) The President has been known to display narcissistic behavior and an exaggerated feeling of self-importance during his pronouncements.

(5) Our President seems to believe the ends justify the means.

(6) One never knows if the President thinks everything is part of one big game he is playing. Maybe this is a part of a master plan to either gain or maintains power or influence.

(7) To the President credit, he relishes in pushing his adversaries' buttons and has no problem doing so. The President seems to believe control and manipulation are just tactics which can be useful for getting an individual to do what he wants them to do.

(8) President Trump relishes in being respected and loved by his supporters but not at the expense of losing respect.

(9) President Trump does not reveal the entire reason for what he is doing or is saying something unless it is to his advantage.

(10) The President seems to enjoy when people seemingly appear to be unaware of the whole picture and in his reality, they are.

   (1)   When things are going well it is all photo-op and smiles.

   (2)   Exhibits duplicitous behavior and can be deceitful (lying).

   (3)   Appears cunning (a crafty use of wellness and trickery)

   (4)   Displays narcissistic behavior. Has an excessive and exaggerated feeling of self-importance, even though these feeling often

   (5)   Believe the ends justify the means.

(6) Believe everything is part of one big game they are playing. And this type of leader it's all part of the master plan to either gain or maintain power or influence

(7) Knows how to push someone button and d have no problems pushing them. In addition, this type of leaders, believes control and manipulation are just tactics.

(8) Loves to be loved but not at the expense of not being feared or respected.

(9) Does not reveal the entire reason they're doing or saying something unless it somehow is to their advantages. They always enjoy it when individuals behave like they are missing part of the whole picture, actually you are.

If this management style reminds you of President Trump, you are probably on the right track. The Commander-in-Chiefs' behavior more closely resembles the type of management style referred to as Machiavellian Leadership Style. The next question for some of you is who was Machiavellian? Niccolo Machiavellian was born on May 3, 1469 in Florence, Italy. He was an Italian Renaissance political philosopher and statesman and secretary of the Florentine Republic. His famous work was the book called, "The Prince".

If you related the Machiavellian Leadership Style to our Commander-In-Chief, you may be on to something. Why, because millions of Americans are questioning why the President is divisive and often use name-calling tactics as a form of communication. Sometimes it seems as if he is alienating his fellow Republicans and most of the Democrats in Congress. The President lied 1,318 times since being president. He always tends to be boastful about his greatness. Our President dipple and dapple in divisiveness. He is likely managing this way to maintain power and support from his base. The calling pattern and insulting people may be just a strategy he finds entertaining. The President always attacks the press by referring to them as FAKE NEWS. Unfortunately, his opposition may relate this tactic to a governing style associated with dictators. The question becomes whether this leadership style can help President Trump push his political agenda?

Well it very simple, the President is trying to run the country using the same management style he used in his successful real estate development business.

The problem is the United States government platform is based on democratic principles. The government is not run like a business because you have three distinct components; Executive, Legislative and Judicial; all with equal power. Although the president is the Commander-in-Chief and responsible for daily operations of the United States government, there are checks-and-balances that he is subjected to by the United States Congress and the Judicial Branches. **Democracy** is a system of rule by laws, not by individuals. In a **democracy**, the rule of law protects the rights of citizens, maintains order, and limits the power **government**. All citizens are equal under the law. No one is above the law, not even the President.

Constitution of the United States Preamble

United States Constitution Amendments 1ˢᵗ and 12ᵗʰ

"We the People of the United States of America"

We the People of the United States, *in order to form a more perfect Union, establish Justice, insure domestic Tranquility, provide for the common defense, promote the general Welfare, and secure the Blessings of Liberty to ourselves and our Posterity, do ordain and establish this Constitution for the United States of America."*

We the People means; the people gives the government its power. Therefore, the President and Congress are responsible for doing the People's 'work, and looking out for the interest of the all the citizens, and not just the interest of a few.

We the People of the United States is such a powerful and profound statement; because it" immediately affirms that the Constitution is of the people, for the people, and by the people of the United States

The constitution is a set of fundamental principles or established precedents that outline the right and responsibilities of citizens of the United States.

1st Amendment to the United States Constitution
Regarding the Rights of the People

The 1st amendment states that Congress shall make no law respecting an establishment of religion, or prohibiting the free exercise thereof; or abridging the freedom of speech, or of the press; or the *right of* the *people* peaceably to *assemble*, and to petition the government for a redress of grievances.

12th Amendment to the United States Constitution
Regarding Electoral Votes

The 12th amendment is the most misunderstood component of the constitution. Why, because this modification is used to establish voting rights and protocols when a presidential candidate wins the popular vote but not the elector/electoral votes. This amendment played a significant role in the 2016 election where Senator Clinton won 65,316,724 popular votes, and Trump won 62,719, 568 votes, giving Senator Clinton a marginal lead 2.6 million. However, she did not win because of the 12th Amendment of Constitution which states you have to win a specific number of electoral votes to become President of the United States. Senator Clinton won 227 while Candidate Trump won 304 electoral votes.

Media Coverages of the 2016 Election

"President Trump must have made millions for new agency before and after his election."

The media coverage was off the hook during the 2016 election and unprecedented. There were 24 hours of coverage for both candidates. CNN, MSNBC, CSPAN, FOX NEWS, CNBC, Bloomberg Television, and Fox Business Network devoted countless hours on interviews, commentary, discussions, and predictions on Senator Clinton and Mr. Trump campaign. These TV mediums seemed to be in a TV rating war. However, there appeared to be more catastrophic coverage regarding Trump as opposed to Hillary.

Media coverage of both candidates was excessive. Every news story referenced either Donald Trump or Senator Hillary Clinton in its headline. The New York Times, The Washington Post, Chicago Tribune, Wall Street Journal, Slate, Politico, Fox News and CNN, seemed to be in a media war. Whether the outlet was liberal or conservative, the American public consumed a daily dose of the candidates via a 24hrs news cycle. The coverage was either about who did what, who said what and who misrepresented the truth and why. It was like people watching their favorite reality TV show or their favorite soap opera. In terms of the print media, everyone started utilizing their individual digital devices to keep up with election campaign events.

The tone of the coverage indicated that one candidate was getting the shorter end of the deal. For example, Donald Trump's worst weeks came in November 2015. This was around the time he suggested the need for a national database on Muslim citizens and mocked a disabled New York Times reporter. The tone of Clinton's media coverage suffered most when her private email server scandal came to the forefront once again in early July 2016.

If candidate Donald Trump felt his message or positions were misstated or misrepresented, he immediately converted to using social media. He was the first Presidential candidate who mastered the art of getting his position out utilizing various forms of social media. Regarding candidates getting their message out, the way it happened in 2015 and 2016, it was a groundbreaking use of the internet social media tools. Mr. Trump also had an excellent game plan for using social media.

He tweeted late at night or in the wee hours of the morning. Mr. Trump mastered the art of controlling statements or comments made by the media. To his credit, he was able to reiterate his message 24/7. Even though Senator Clinton used social media her campaign advisors seemingly weren't as savvy using social media as a political instrument as her opponent. In the final analyses, it is evident that the majority of Americans, especially young people got most of the information from the internet or cell phones.

Economic Systems

"Definition of an Economic System: Is a system wherein the government organized ways in which money, goods and services are allocated".

Few Americans understand the difference between capitalism, socialism and communism and how these systems work as economic systems. Furthermore, most American has an unconscious fear of these two systems of governing and see them as the bogeymen in the closet. Americans are comfortable with capitalism, even though they do not have a clear, definitive understanding of this economic system. Capitalism is the economic system

Americans interact with on a daily basis. Senator Clinton and President Trump are capitalists. However, Senator Bernie Sanders is a democratic socialist.

"Is it all about the Benjamins"?

Some Americans understand that they live in a capitalist society, while others do not. Even though they know they live in a capitalist country, millions of Americans do not understand how our economic system works. Therefore, to make capitalism more palpable, politicians, businesspeople, and corporations refer to capitalism as a free enterprise system. So let's take a historical look at the philosopher of capitalism and how it works.

Did you know capitalism is an economic theory and philosophy developed by Adam Smith (1723-1790)? In a capitalist system all or most of the means of production and distribution are control by wealthy business people and large corporations. In a capitalist society, these individuals determine how to organize material resources and the cost of these materials. Wealthy businessmen and women are considered members of the ruling class or wealthy elite class.

These are the people who control the means of production within societies.

They are investors in monetary purchases that they resale to the general public for an excessive profit. Real estate moguls like Trump are considered capitalists.

There is an economic system called, "Democratic Capitalism" which is based on a free marketplace and monetary incentives. This type of financial structure is supposed to established moral traditions to encourage diversity. Democratic capitalism is a combination of three systems: (a) free markets and economic incentives (b) commercial organizations and (c) a financial system that encourages diversity. Furthermore, in a democratic economic order, there are checks and balances that prohibit the large corporations or businesses from exploiting the masses. Unfortunately, property rights, monetary justice and revenue motivations, competition and the division of labor are all controlled by the rich and powerful.

Socialism and Democratic Socialism

Socialism originated in the late 18th century and early 19th century-- the result of economic and social changes linked to the Industrial Revolution. Henri de Saint-Simon coined the term socialism. Socialism is defined as equality in the society, and democratic socialism means justice in a democratic state. However, other significant thinkers who focused on the economy believed in the application of modern technology for rationalizing economic systems. Socialists are critics of private ownership.

Socialism is an economic structure that the government owns or controls significant industries. The definition of socialism varies widely and is a financial system that is said to be the child of communism and capitalism. Socialism seeks to redistribute the wealth more equitably by the communal ownership of natural resources and primary industries such as banking and public utilities. Socialism is also a system of collective ownership and management of the means of production and the distribution of goods. Socialists believe that in capitalism, the wealth and power are concentrated in a small section of the society.

"Senator Sanders' political campaign might have been more successful if Americans did not fear Socialism, Democratic Socialism or Communism. Many Americans see Socialism and Communism as the bogeymen in the closet".

Senator Sanders, a Democratic Socialist, did not become the democratic nominee for President in 2016 because people were afraid of the term socialism.

However, he played a significant role in the primary election. Sanders captured the attention of many millennials, mostly young whites and majorities between the ages of 18-34 in 2015/2016. Senator Sanders has been a Democratic Socialist since 2007.

To understand Sander's political platform and ideology one must appreciate Democratic Socialism. Sanders advocated for a society that included social ownership of the means of production, with an emphasis on democratic management of enterprises within a democratic socialist system. The fundamental difference between socialism and democratic socialism is socialists do not want the government to own the primary means of production and believe for example, health care systems should be controlled by the government.

People identify Senator Sanders as a Democratic Socialist, but many people do not know that one of most profound freedom fighters in the United States was Dr. Martin Luther King who was also considered a Democratic Socialist.

Communism

What is Communism? To understand communism, one would have to contrast the differences between capitalism and democratic socialism. Karl Marx and Friedrich Engels wrote The "Communist Manifesto on February 21, 1848", which was published in London by Marx and Engels who were German revolutionaries. Their political party was the Communist League. Marx and Engel felt that millions of working-class people were fed up with being exploited by the middle class and upper class. The "Communist Manifesto" asserted that class struggle was indicative of the hate the ruling class has for the working class. To put to rest the working class problems that existed in Germany; Marx and Engle believed there had to be a political victory for the proletariat meaning (working class) to generate an inevitable victory for the working class.

Most Americans do not understand and are fearful of communism. Americans have a fear and mistrust of all communist countries and the leadership of these countries. Therefore, to have a dialogue about economic systems, one must discuss and debate communism as an industrial infrastructure. In a communist country, the government decides what products are produced, sold and the cost of these commodities. Whereas, in a capitalist society, the decisions of who provides what, when and how, is left to the corporations and businesses.

Poverty in America

Poverty in the Richest Country in the World

Many Americans do not know that in 2015, approximately 45 million Americans were living in poverty. What is shocking about millions of American living in poverty is America is supposed to be the wealthiest country in the World. According to the U.S. Census, the official poverty rate was 13.5 percent 2015. Also, based on Census data, an estimated 43.1 million Americans lived in poverty.

*"If America is the richest country in the world; how can there
be so many poor people —can this be an oxymoron?"*

Many different factors cause poverty in America, drug abuse, violence, oppression, lack of education, and income disparity. It has been argued that the structural aspect of a capitalistic system might play a role in the construct of who accumulates wealth and who do not.

Rust Belt States Put Donald Trump in the White House

"Was poverty, drugs and high unemployment the catalyst for Candidate Trump winning the 2016 Election?

Poverty, drug addiction, and high unemployment levels helped President Trump win the 2016 election. Why, because the Rust Belt States suffered from an economic decline due to industrial deterioration and the transfer or loss of manufacturing plants. Another factor to consider was automation and the ability to produce products that were once generated by human workers. Furthermore, there was a decline in the steel and coal industries. In some areas throughout the rust belt people did not adapt to the industrial decline and focused their attention on high-tech industries. For the people who did not change, this caused a population decline and a rise in poverty. Mrs. Kelly Ann Conway, Trump's campaign manager, encouraged Mr. Trump, to hold many rallies in the Rust Belt states. "The rust belt states were the unforeseen elephant in the room for Senator Clinton campaign." The Rust Belt States that helped President Trump win the election were Pennsylvania, Ohio, Michigan, West Virginia and Wisconsin. As of 2016, approximately 50,000 Americans have died from drug overdose in many of this area. "Did you know that President Obama won many of these states in 2008 and 2012"?

Blue = Number of people in America and orange = number in poverty in 205

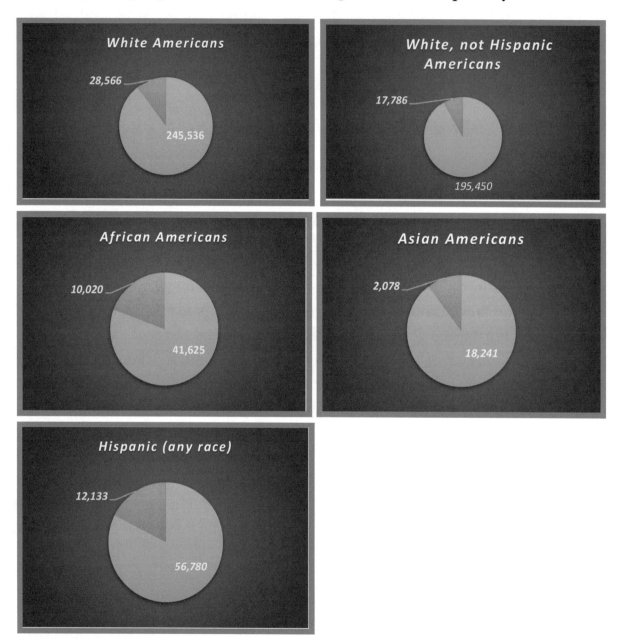

White Americans
28,566
245,536

White, not Hispanic Americans
17,786
195,450

African Americans
10,020
41,625

Asian Americans
2,078
18,241

Hispanic (any race)
12,133
56,780

Statistical Data Source: U.S. Censors

Poverty in America–Income Levels Based on Household Size

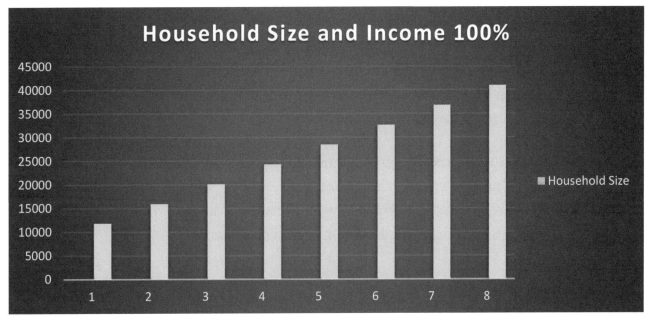

Statistical Data Source: Department of Health & Human Services (HHS)

Class Structures in America

Why is it important to understand class structures in America? Well, it played a role in helping President Trump win the 2016 election. Also, it gave people insight into why Senator Clinton did not gain some of these voters support; even though, President Obama did well in 2008 and 2012. Class structures is related to economic standing within a country. You have the poor, working, lower-middle, upper-middle, and upper class (the wealthy are referred to as the establishment or elite class).

The lower class consists of those who are at the bottom of the socioeconomic ladder. They are individuals with minimal education, limited income, and low-status jobs and typically work positions that are not prestigious and require limited skills. If they become unemployed, they usually apply for government assistance. The working class consists of individuals who perform blue-collar work. Middle class white collar workers usually have high school diplomas, a college degree, and perform semi-professional work. The upper middle class work in professional positions and have higher education degrees such as a bachelor or master degree. Upper class groups of individuals acquire jobs as doctors, lawyers, and executives. Many become entertainers. Their children attend private schools and Ivy League private colleges.

Why are class structures critical to understand in term of the election in 2016? Because, it was the poor, working and middle class from the Rust Belt who put President Trump in the Whitehouse. Not because they agreed with everything he said or did, it was because he was smart enough to address their economic and class issues.

Drugs and the 2016 Election

Why was the drug epidemic mentioned by all the presidential candidates in the 2016 presidential election? The problem is so apparent that one cannot stroll through any poor or working class neighborhood and not witness drug addicts patrolling the streets in just about every city in America (especially at night) looking for their next fix. These individuals remind you of the walking dead. There are many reasons why more Americans than ever are using an illegal drug. It could be poverty, cultural attitude toward narcotics or the opioid crises. Nevertheless, Americans are consuming drugs at an unprecedented rate in America.

The Drug Epidemic in America

Illegal drug use in the U.S. is reaching epidemic levels. In 2013, one million Americans were illicit drug users, about 9.4 percent of the population aged 12 or older; this is up from the 2002-09 rate of 7.9 percent. The drugs used included marijuana/hashish, cocaine/crack, heroin, hallucinogens, inhalants and prescription-type psychotherapeutics. Among whites, illicit drug use increased to 9.5 percent from 8.5 percent in less than a decade.

Illegal drugs have evolved from the inner cities (i.e., black crime) to a suburban (i.e., white) disease. A 2015 Gallup poll of the use of "mood altering drugs" found that seven of the top 10 states with the highest level of abuse – the percent of those using "almost every day" – were red states located in the South: West Virginia (28.1%), Kentucky (24.5%), Alabama (24.2%), Louisiana (22.9%), South Carolina (22.8%), Mississippi (22.3%) and Missouri (22.2%).

The change in the character of illegal drug use is no better expressed than in the personal tragedies experienced of two former Republican presidential candidates, Carly Fiorina and Jeb Bush.

Rosen, D. (n.d.). Illegal Drugs, Race and the 2016 Elections-Counterpunch. http://www.counterpunch.org/2016/03/18/illegal-drugs-race-and-the-2018-elections/

The National Institutes of Health found that from 2001 to 2014 the U. S. witnessed a threefold increase in deaths due to opioid pain relievers and a six-fold increase in heroin overdoses. During the same period, overdose deaths from prescription drugs like Valium and Klonopin — sedatives called benzodiazepines — increased fivefold.

The Centers for Disease Control (CDC) notes that overdoses (i.e., "drug poisoning") are "the number one cause of injury-related death in the United States, with 43,982 deaths occurring in 2013." Studies show based on data from 28 states, the "death rate for heroin overdose doubled from 2010 through 2012." Drilling down, it found there were 8,257 heroine deaths, most involving men aged 25–44 years.

Rosen, D. (n.d.). Illegal Drugs, Race and the 2016 Elections-Counterpunch.
http://www.counterpunch.org/2016/03/18/illegal-drugs-race-and-the-2018-elections/

In 2013, whites had the highest suicide rate in the country, at 14.2 per 100,000; American Indians and Alaska Natives were second with a rate of 11.7. However, during 2005–2009, the highest suicide rates were among American Indian/Alaskan Native males with 27.6 suicides and non-Hispanic white males with 25.96 suicides. Among women, non-Hispanic whites had the highest rate with 6.7 suicides. Illegal drugs, the prison-industrial complex and the changing racial character of addiction – and suicide – surfaced a couple of times during the 2016 presidential race. Republicans and Democrats spoke out about America drug addiction problem.

Rosen, D. (n.d.). Illegal Drugs, Race and the 2016 Elections-Counterpunch.
http://www.counterpunch.org/2016/03/18/illegal-drugs-race-and-the-2018-elections/

Republican Candidates Position on Drugs

Ted Cruz (Senator, TX) favors harsh mandatory minimum sentences for nonviolent drug crimes. "When it comes to a question of legalizing marijuana, I don't support legalizing marijuana. If it were on the ballot in the state of Texas, I would vote no. But I also believe that's a legitimate question for the states to make a determination…I think it is appropriate for the federal government to recognize that the citizens of those states have made that decision, and one of the benefits of it according to the Supreme Court Justice

Louis Brandeis' terms of "Laboratories of Democracy", is we can now watch and see what happens in Colorado and Washington State."

John Kasich (governor, OH) opposes the legalization of marijuana for medical and recreational purposes, but considers it a states' rights issue. "If I happened to be president, I would lead a significant campaign down at the grassroots level to stomp these drugs out of our country."

Donald Trump, (NY) supports legalization of medical marijuana, but opposes legalization for recreational purposes. "I say it's bad. … Medical marijuana is another thing, but I think recreational marijuana is bad. And I feel strongly about that." He also supports state's rights to decide: "If they vote for it, they vote for it. But they've got a lot of problems going on right now, in Colorado. Some big problems, but I think medical marijuana, 100 percent."

Rosen, D. (n.d.). Illegal Drugs, Race and the 2016 Elections – Counterpunch.
http://www.counterpunch.org/2016/03/18illegal-drugs-race-and-2016-elctions

Democratic Candidates:
The two Democratic candidates reflect a more nuanced stand on illegal drugs, each calling for a greater emphasis on prevention, treatment and recovery as well as revision of criminal prosecution. The following quotes are from their respective websites.

Hillary Clinton (former Sec. of State, NY) supported use of medical marijuana and for states to regulate recreational use. "I do support the use of medical marijuana, and I think even there we need to do a lot more research so that we know exactly how we're going to help people for whom medical marijuana provides relief." "I think that we have the opportunity through the states that are pursuing recreational marijuana to find out a lot more than we know today."

Bernie Sanders (Senator, VT) took the most progressive stand on illegal drugs, calling for nonviolent drug offenders to receive treatment instead of incarceration. He supported medical use of marijuana and more study of Colorado's recreational use of marijuana. With regard to growing the heroin and opioid epidemic, he's called for "preventative measures to increase education and rehabilitation in order to combat this epidemic."

Bernie Sanders supports the medical use of marijuana and the rights of states to determine its legality. He co-sponsored the States' Rights to Medical Marijuana Act in 2001." "Vermont voted to decriminalize the possession of small amounts of marijuana and I support that."

Rosen, D. (n.d.). Illegal Drugs, Race and the 2016 Elections – Counterpunch. http://www.counterpunch.org/2016/03/18illegal-drugs-race-and-2016-elctions/.

Political Institutions in America

"Different Strokes for Different Folks"

In America, there are different political institutions such as the Democrat, Republican, Libertarian, Socialist and Communist Parties. What this means is a person can be a Democratic, Republican, Libertarian, Socialist or Communist. Are there other political parties? Yes, the Libertarians, Green, and Constitutional Parties. *How would one identify with party affiliation?* Mr. Trump prefers to be called a conservative republican, Senator Clinton is a Democrat and Senator Bernie Sanders is a Democratic Socialist.

Political **Philosophies**

How do people identify with a candidate's beliefs system? Referred to as a candidate's political ideology, it's the reason why one voter may vote for one candidate, while their neighbor may vote for another candidate. Most candidates have a platform that identifies whether he or she is a liberal, conservative, socialist, democrat or republican. Understanding a candidates' political philosophy is necessary because it gives the perspective voters reasons or ideas why they should vote for a candidate of their chose.

A look at political groups in the United States, such as Liberals (Left) Moderate (Middle) and Conservative (Right) Let's examine these political ideologies more closely.

| Left | | Middle | | Right |

Liberalism Left-Political Ideology-What they "Believes"

Liberals believe in equal opportunity for all and do not support racism, sexism, religion, age, disabilities and sexual orientation discrimination. This ideology has always had roots in the Democratic Party. Liberals have a problem with the disparity of wealth and the inequalities between the wealthy and the have-nots. Civil rights and liberal values are important to the libertarians.

They supported President Obama's Affordable Healthcare Act. Another component of their platform is quality and affordable education for all. Libertarians are believers in the Environmental Clean Air Act. This Leftist group believes that social programs are necessary for disadvantaged and unemployed Americans. They embrace "Affirmative Action" and believe in the workers' rights to organize and strike when exploited by their employers. Furthermore, their belief system encompasses health and safety protection for all employees. Liberals advocates for a progressive tax system that taxes citizens based on their income.

Conservative-Right-Political Ideology-What they "Believe".

Conservatives believe the best way to develop individual rights is through smaller government. Most conservatives are republicans. They are not enthusiastic about bringing about change in public policy. They prefer as little government intervention as possible along with dynamic leadership. Conservatives base their philosophy on religious teachings, such as morality. They prefer to tone down the rational social programs proposed by secular theorists, economists, and the intelligentsia in the society. They are anti-abortion, affirmative action programs and workers' labor unions. Conservatives have no problems with inequalities of income. They support the status quo and privilege class within a society. They also have limited concerns or difficulties with some people having more rights or better opportunities than others. They are egalitarian and technically are not disturbed by the disparity of social and economic standings of individuals in the society.

Moderates-Middle-Political Ideology-What they "Believe"

Moderate or middle of the road voters, support both liberals and conservative ideologies. These individuals can also be considered swing voters. They prefer to be thought of as moderates.

Communism-Far/Left-Political Ideology-What they "Believe"

The people who support this type of ideology have a tendency to believe in communal proprietorship of property and most businesses within their society. In a communist country, the majority of the population has access to free health care, even if it's not the best healthcare.

In these societies, the people in power believe the means of production and distribution should be regulated and controlled by the government (people in authority at any given time). Furthermore, this type of ideology advocates for an economic infrastructure that supposedly guards the interest of the populace. However, the government controls the media and has strict rules against anti-government rhetoric or demonstrations.

Socialism-Left-Political Ideology-What they "Believe".

Socialists believe there is an alternative to capitalism. Corporations should not be in control of goods and services within a society. Also, the natural resources should be maintained. Furthermore, they believe in democratic socialism. Socialists are advocates for civil liberties and democracy.

National Socialism-Alt Right Political Ideology (Nazism)-What they "Believe"

National Socialism ideology was established in some European countries, after World War I. People who practice this doctrine do not respect liberals, democracy and human rights. The government officials and Nationalists believe their people should be subordinate to their appointed leaders. Also, the agents of the state feel they have the right to rule the weaker members of the society. The leadership in many countries that practice National Socialism don't believe in the equality of individuals and adhere to racial superiority of White Anglo-Saxons. They feel they have the right to control the means of production, economic development, the political arena and institutions of higher education. Nevertheless, they do adhere to free health care for their citizens. The most known politician was Adolf Hitler; who gave birth to the National Socialist German Workers' Party after WWI.

Fascism-Extreme Right-Political Ideology (Nazism)-What they "Believe"

Fascists' political ideology adheres to the extreme rule of the state. Fascists believe in active young people, spiritual unity, and extreme violence. They do not believe in democracy, socialism or capitalism. Fascists believe government has the right to take extreme measures to control the people within their society. They have no problem conducting surveillance on their citizens. They believe that those in power have the absolute duty to ensure people adhere to the laws and dictator's power. Fascists believe in racist superiority, ethnic persecutions, imperialist expansion, and genocide.

Furthermore, they believe the government or ruling party is more superior to the ordinary citizens. They believe human rights are not important and freedom of speech technically is not welcome in this type of political atmosphere. They believe that the citizen has no right to protest the government or participate in a political demonstration. Also, protesting against the government is dangerous. In many cases, protesters are imprisoned, and dissenters tend to disappear under authoritarian governments.

Anarchism-Racial Left Political Ideology-What they "Believe"

Anarchists believe in a stateless society. They think central governing is not necessary and harmful and believe in a society that is self-governed by the people. This group is also anti-authoritarian and rejects all political ideologies. The also feel human being should rely on authority to conduct relationships between people. Anarchism can be confusing because Anarchists believe in extreme individualism or either collectivism, which seem to be a contradiction. Furthermore, Anarchists appears to believe in an anti-authoritarian interpretation communism, socialism, and participatory economic.

Libertarianism- Left- Political Ideology-What they "Believe"

This political philosophy is fundamentally new and gained popularity in the 20th century. Libertarians believe that individual rights are at the forefront of any legitimate government. Libertarians adhere to a free and prosperous world and feel that politicians should not utilize deception that impedes societal relationships. They are advocates of freedom, peace, and prosperity. They also believe diversity comes along with freedom. Libertarians embrace the idea that individuals should be free to follow their dreams without interference from government or any authoritarian power. They also feel people have the right to free speech and the state should not impede freedom of expression or media. Additionally, Libertarians do not support government censorship and oppose government hindrance of private property. Therefore, they object to government officials confiscating any individual's property. They do not believe in nationalization and the eminent domain policy. They are against government restraints and regulations in the areas of economic and non-economic entities that pertain to citizens' livelihood.

Marxism- Left- Political Ideology-What they "Believe"

Karl Marx and Frederick Engle wrote "The Communist Manifesto". Marx felt that capitalism was the root of all evils and class divisions within democratic systems. Marxists are a worker's party organization and feel the means of production should be controlled by workers' unions. Their ideology is based on Marx's "Dialectical Materialism" theory which explains the historical relationship between material forces that are in conflict, therefore, creating many contradictions. Marxists believe that people are social beings rather than isolated individuals. They advocate that there is a human activity that mirrors the society in which one lives. Furthermore, Marxists think political systems are grounded in and developed out of economic systems. Some Marxists advocate that a socialist economy is the foundation for a real democracy, even though, other Marxists see democracy as nothing more than a necessary evil. Politically, Marxists see the world as a struggle between the bourgeoisie (owners of private property and the means of production) and the proletariat (workers). In essence, a Marxism belief is that struggle persists in order to control the means of production which will ultimately lead to control of the entire political system within a democracy.

Types of Governing Styles

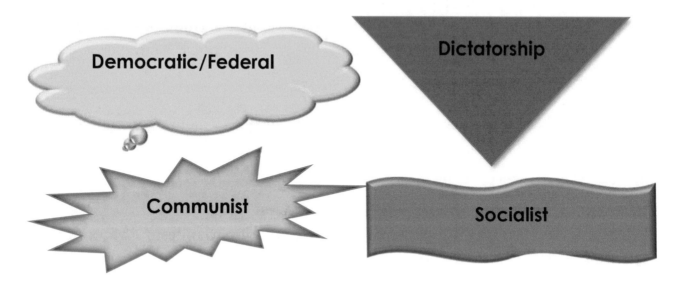

Why Governing Styles Are Important?

Global relations and cooperation between countries are essential in today's world. States governing styles have the potential of creating allies or enemies. Therefore, it is necessary to generate a discussion on the various governing styles that exist in the world today. In fact, governing styles were points of discussion throughout the 2016 Presidential campaign.

The United States of America is a federal government within a democratic society. Why? There are federal, state and local governing styles that are in place to protect the interests and security of the citizens. Another way to look at governing styles is to examine ways in which citizens participate. For example, in the United States, government officials are elected by the people. City, state, and federal elections are held every two - three years.

On the national level, you have three branches in place to protect the interest of the citizenry through a check and balance system. They are as follows: Executive (President), Legislative (Senate and House of Representatives who make up the Congress), and Judicial (Supreme Court and Lower Courts).

America is not isolated from the world as having a democratic government. In fact, there are several countries that implement democratic principles like the United States which are listed below. It is significant to note that some of these governments have not always been democratic societies.

The governing style of the Russian Federation consists of executive, legislative and judicial branches. The president is sometimes referred to as the Chief of Staff and represents the executive branch. This position is one of substantial power, and the legislature is subordinate to the executive branch. Like other democracies, Russia has a constitution and voters elect their president every four years. The most important difference between the United States governing vs. the Russian governing style is that the United States governs from the bottom up wherein Russia governs from the top down.

Some samples of some countries that use the democratic governing style:

Countries that have Democratic/Federal Governing Style in the 21st Century			
United States	Dominican Republic	Germany	India
Kingdom of the Netherlands	Russia*	Mexico	Pakistan

*D*ictatorship/*A*uthoritarian *Government Style*

A dictatorship or authoritarian is a governing style where one individual or political entity utilizes various mechanisms to gain control over the government. In the 21st century, dictators do not refer to themselves as dictators instead they tend to give themselves titles such as president, prime ministers, or chancellors. Usually, the country is governed by one person with no checks or balances. Most dictators seize power through violent struggle or a revolution. Some of the most unpopular dictators were; Adolf Hitler, Mao Zedong. Idi Amin, Saddam Hussein, Joseph Stalin and Pol Pot just to name a few.

In a dictatorial or authoritarian style of government, there may or may not be elections or a democratic accountability structure. In some cases, presidential elections exist, and opposition parties may be allowed to participate. However, they hold virtually no power in government.

Also, this type governing style tends to suppress any political opposition. The dictator immediately takes controls of major institutions. Also, this kind of governing style has complete control over the citizenry. Another component is the dictator usually engage in attacking their predecessor(s) through the media or at political rallies. This strategy is used to minimize the political achievements of their predecessor. In many cases, the dictators have been known to participate in ethnic cleansing, deportation, and mass murders.

The majority of the political policies are developed by the authoritarian/dictator. This type of leadership rarely consults with other branches of the government, when making policy decisions. Governmental offices are usually controlled by an autocrat. Any questioning of policies or political decisions can result in imprisonment, exile or assassination. Repressive dictators do not have high favorability level. One must note that there are countries in the 21st century that still live under a dictatorial governing style. In some of these countries, there are multiple ruling styles because they can be referred to as communist countries or states and may or may not be entirely controlled by the dictators.

Some samples of some countries that use the authoritarian governing style

Countries that have Dictators/Authoritarian Governing Style in the 21ˢᵗ Century				
Belarus	Cambodia	Cameroon	Chad	Egypt
Equatorial Guinea	Eritrea	Myanmar	Iran	Kazakhstan

Communists Governing Style

Communist governing style utilizes a central state platform, wherein most private enterprise and businesses are controlled by the government.

A communist state is referred to as a one-party system. The Prime Minister or President is the public face of the country. Industrial markets and agriculture are state-run. This type of governing style usually provides all education, healthcare, and welfare. The social classes include: lower, middle and upper class. Equality of wages and other amenities are kept consistent throughout the society.

However, in today's communist states, there exists an elite class, which is rarely discussed. Additionally, this governing style allows for political participation involving other non-party organizations such as trade unions and factory committees. Some of these governments do not refer to themselves as communist states, instead they are called Socialist or Workers' states. *See table below:*

Some samples of some countries that use the communist governing style

Countries that have Communist Governing Style in the 21st Century			
Cuba	Laos	North Korea	North Vietnam

Socialist Governing Style

Socialist governing styles vary from country to country. They have two-party or multi-party systems and conduct elections. The government may consist of a President and Prime Minister. Today, socialist governments have legislative and judicial branches. In most of these countries, political ideologies and theories are aimed at establishing social ownership and democratic control of the means of production. Most socialist governments have free healthcare for all of their citizens.

Some samples of some countries that use the socialist governing style

Countries that have Socialist Governing Style in the 21st Century				
Belgium	Canada	China	Denmark	Finland
Ireland	Netherland	New Zealand	Norway	Sweden

United State Governmental Structure Have Three Different Branches

The Executive, Legislative and Judicial

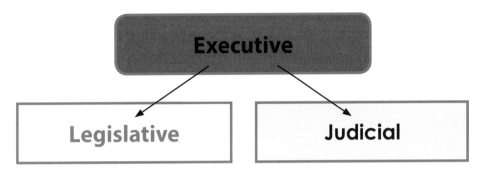

"The constitution divided the government into three different branches to ensure the separation of power. No single branch has control of the other; thereby Creating of a System of Checks and Balances."

Executive Branch

The President controls the executive branch. The President oversees the Vice President, Cabinet Members, Advisors, and Heads of Independent Agencies. The President is the Commander in Chief and can create and sign executive orders. He or she can sign as many executive orders they want. These requests can be directed towards officers and agencies of the Federal government. Executive orders do have the full power of law, enforced by the authority derived from statutes of the Constitution. However, even though an executive order is a law, they can be reversed by the Courts and Congress.

Legislative Branch

This branch referred to as the United States Congress. The Congress consists of the House of Representatives and the Senate. The Congress is made up of both Democrats and Republicans. The House leadership is referred to as the Speaker of the House. There are two leaders in the Senate; Senate Majority and Minority Leaders. Congress has two leaders Majority and Minority leaders. The legislation is a bill and is voted on by the House of Representative and Senate. If the majority of the Representatives of the House and Senate votes to approve the new legislation, the President then signs the bills into law. Federal courts may review this legislation and strike it down if they think the legislation does not meet the articles of the Constitution.

Judicial Branch

The Supreme Court has nine justices that sit on the court, and they are appointed for life. This branch of the government consists of a Chief Justice, and eight judges known as Associate Justices. Presidents can nominate a judge; however, the judge must be confirmed by the Senate. The Supreme Court is the main body of the judicial branch. This branch consists of the criminal and civil courts. The judiciary uses its unique power known as judicial review, known as the check and balance between the three branches of the federal government. Once the Supreme Court liberates a case, no other court can challenge it. The responsibility of the Supreme Court is to view a case released by the lower courts and interpret the legality of the case based on the Constitution of the United States.

United States Congress

United States Congress, is comprised of the House of Representatives (Republicans and Democrats), and the Senate consists of (Republicans and Democrats). Sometimes in the House and the Senate, Republicans vote with the Democrats on legislations, and sometimes Democrats support Republicans on legislations. Each party holds a certain amount of seats in the House and the Senate, based on the results of elections for each state. The responsibility of Congress is to write, debate, and pass laws (legislation), which are sent to the president for his or her approval and final signature.

The House of Representatives

"House of Representatives serve two-year terms and must run for reelection during an even-numbered year such as 2018, 2020 or 2022."

The Honorable Paul Davis Ryan Jr., a Republican, is the 54th Speaker of the House of Representatives and the Presiding Officer. The Speaker of the House duties include administering the oath of office to members, calling the House to order, maintaining order and decorum within the House chamber and galleries, acknowledging members who want to speak on the House floor and making judgments about policies and procedures. The Speaker of the House does not vote but he can cast a vote if there is a tie. Members of the House of Representatives serve two-year terms and are considered for reelection every even year.

There are party leaders and whips of the United States House of Representatives, who are considered floor leaders. They are elected by their respective parties in a closed-door caucus, which is a secret ballot. The leadership consists of the Majority Leader, Kevin McCarthy, Majority Whip, Steven Scalise, Minority Leader Nancy Pelosi, and Minority Whip Steny Hoyer. The United States House of Representatives use the terms Republican Leader or Democratic Leader.

(a) Party whip is an official of a political party whose task is to ensure party discipline during legislative sessions.

(b) The leader of the minority party conduct business on the floor of either the Senate or the House of Representatives.

Republicans vs. Democrats Seats in the House of Representatives

Republicans 238	Democrats 193	Vacancies 4

"The party that controls the most seats usually controls legislative votes".
However, sometimes Republicans vote with Democrats and Vice Vera".

The Senate

"Each state elects two senators to serve six-year terms which
means every six years they must run for re-election".

The Senate is part of the Congress; it consists of a group of elected officials who decide the laws of the country. Every state elects two people to represent them in the U.S. Senate. These elective officials are called Senators. The Senate and the House of Representatives are responsible for all lawmaking done by Congress. For an act of Congress to be valid, both House of Representatives and Senate must vote to approve the legislation or law.

Vice President Pence is considered the Presiding Officer of the United States Senate. However, Vice Presidents cannot vote in the Senate, except to break a tie. Nor can he/she formally address the Senate, except with the senators' permission. Some of the duties of the Senate include: writing and passing laws, approving many presidential appointments, and ratifying treaties with other countries.

Republicans vs. Democrats Seats in the Senate

Republicans 54	Democrats 48

"The party that controls the most seats usually controls legislative votes".
However, sometimes Republicans vote with Democrats and Vice Vera

Legislative Process

<u>Article I, Section 1, of the United States Constitution</u>

"All Legislative Powers herein granted shall be vested in a Congress of the United States, which shall consist of a Senate and House of Representatives."

Any member in the House of Representatives may introduce a bill at any time while the House is in session by simply placing it in the "hopper" (a brown box) at the side of the Clerk's desk in the House Chamber, The most important phase of the legislative process is the action taken by committees.

How Laws are Passed?

A law is an idea that representatives can sponsor. It goes to a committee for study. If released it is then voted on, debated or amended. If the bill passes by a small majority (218 of 435), the concept moves to the Senate. If it leaves the Senate with no questions or concerns, the potential law goes to another committee. When it is released, it is debated, brought to the floor for a vote. To become a bill, it will require a small majority (51 of 100). Finally, a group of representatives and senators works on any differences. House and Senate may or may not present another version of the legislation. The concept or idea (law) is delivered to the House and Senate for approval. The Government Printing Office prints the final bill. Finally, the Commander-in-Chief signs the new legislation within ten days or vetoes the document.

Presidential Candidate, Senator Hillary Rodman-Clinton's Campaign Message of 2016

"Hillary Won The Popular Votes; The Question Become How And Why She Lost the 2016 Election?"

Senator Hillary Rodman Clinton (The First Lady of the White House from (1993-2005)

Hillary started her political career as a young Republican and campaigned for Republican presidential nominee Barry Goldwater in 1964. After hearing a speech by the Reverend Martin Luther King Jr., she became a Democrat in 1968.

Hillary Rodman earned her law degree from Yale University. She married Bill Clinton in 1975 and when Bill Clinton became President in 1993, Hillary functioned as the first lady from 1993 to 2001. She then served as a U.S. senator from 2001 to 2009. In 2007, she decided to run for the presidency. However, at the 2008 Democratic primaries, she conceded when it became apparent that Barack Obama had the majority of the delegate votes. After Obama won the presidency, he appointed Clinton as the secretary of state where she served until 2013. In 2015, Hillary announced her plans to run for president in 2016.

Technically Senator Clinton should have won the 2016 election. She was more experienced and level-headed than her component. Senator Clinton's campaign slogan "Stronger Together" unfortunately did not help her win the 2016 election. It wasn't due to her lack of political experience because she spent 31 years in government. She was an expert on how to articulate policies that would impact millions of American. Senator Clinton's political platform included a wide variety of issues such as: the drug epidemic, economy, campaign finance reform, addressing gun violence legislation, comprehensive immigration reform, racial justice, LGBT rights and equality. She also proposed to make college education affordable and if possible debt free. Hillary's platform was very impressive because it contained other issues that were important to the poor, working class and middle-class Americans.

Senator Hillary Clinton Coalition in 2016

Senator Hillary Rodham Clinton campaigned as a Democrat. Her campaign strategy was to connect with the same young and diverse population that President Obama was able to put together in 2008 and 2012. Hillary wanted to fortify an even more significant component of the female vote than Obama did in 2012. Campaign advisers believed that any social or demographic shifts to the left wouldn't necessarily impact her ability to make the case to the moderate and independent voters in the general election. The campaign relied upon approximately 31 percent of the electorate would be Americans of color. This position, unfortunately, was a little optimistic. The campaign staff believed that a majority of independent voters supported same-sex marriage and a pathway to citizenship for undocumented immigrants that Clinton's general election votes would be somewhat secured.

Some problems embedded with Hillary's campaign platform were paid family leave, a higher minimum wage, and more affordable college education. Her agenda incorporated domestic issues, making her campaign more substantial and gain her more support in 2016 election. However, the strategists did not believe Senator Clinton address liberal voters who were distrustful and concerned about her aggressive attitude on foreign policy.

Hillary's campaign counted on the support of sisterhood. Nonetheless, many women did not embrace the historical significance of the election. The polls showed that many women voted based on their culture and class. However, Senator Clinton' coalition did have the support from one of the most spectacular and beautiful women in modern history, First Lady Michelle Obama.

Senator Clinton had a very impressive campaign agenda and demonstrated superior skills in articulating her political agenda and debating her opponents throughout the campaign. She won the three debates against Mr. Trump. She had a well-thought-out economic plan that would have helped millions of people. Unfortunately, the cloud of scandals that surrounded her campaign made it difficult for her to transition from the past to the future, even though she had more government experience than her component. Regrettably, some severe issues impacted her campaign.

Some of Issues that Impeded Hillary's 2016 campaign

a. The Benghazi scandal, the Clintons foundation scandal
b. President Clinton' sexual controversy
c. The Wiki Leak emails disaster
d. Senator Clinton's inability to mobile young African Americans voters because
e. President Clinton 1994 Violent Crime Control Act
f. Donald Trump campaign statement "draining the swamp"
g. Hillary was seen as a part of the political establishment
h. President Clinton 1996 Welfare Reform Act
i. Senator Clinton position on Black Lives Matter issues and inconsistencies

President Obama Historical Election 2008 and 2012

What happened in 2008 and 2012 was Impossible for Senator Hillary to Overcome

The Historical Framework of President Obama 2008 and 2012 Elections

The 2008 and 2012 elections were historical because Obama was the first African American to become the President of the United State for eight years. Millions of African Americans, progressive whites and people of all nationality consistently voted for this young Senator from Illinois. No matter what his opposition threw at his campaign, the Obama coalition was able to rise above it. Millions of people from every class strata and every walk of life wanted to be part of these historic elections.

Wherever he traveled throughout the United States the crowns were enormous and enthusiastic. Obama won both the popular vote and electoral votes. He also experienced a scandal that could have impeded his run for the Whitehouse. It was the Jeremiah Wright scandal during his first campaign. Reverend Wright was the pastor of the Trinity United Church in Chicago, Illinois. The sermon under question was a speech called, "A More Perfect Union." Many Whites and a few Black Clergymen said the sermon was divisive, which was proven wrong. Then you had the "birther" movement. On January of 2008, Obama became the first African American President of the United States America. In January of 2008, for the first time in American history, an African American family became residents of the Whitehouse.

(Note: *Several Africans attempted a run for President of the United States: Frederick Douglas, George Edwin Taylor, Shirley Chisholm, Jessie Jackson, and Adam Keyes and Dr. Ben Carlson just to name a few*)

Mr. Trump became obsessive with the birther issue for years and demanded in a television interview that President Obama release his birth certificate. At some point, President Obama released his birth certificate to the public, probably to shut Donald Trump up. Did you know if you travel to Hawaii, they will take you on a tour of Obama' old home, the hospital where Obama was born in Honolulu, Hawaii and the schools he attended in Honolulu?

When Obama ran for President for the second time, there were some issues that could have impeded his 2nd campaign. Nevertheless, he won his second term as President in 2012; winning the popular votes and the Electoral College's votes in 2012. Can you guess what states helped Obama win his second term in the Whitehouse? If you say the Rust Belt States, you are correct.

First Lady Michelle Obama Support of Senator Clinton Coalition in 2016

"When They Go Low, We Go High"
By Michelle Obama

Michelle Obama was a fabulous First Lady during the Obama Administration. Many women (especially women of color), felt an enormous sense of pride. Many young women, of all nationalities, began to believe they too could climb to the top of the pinnacle of success. Michelle, in essence, confirmed for many women that they could also be educated, intelligent and beautiful.

The First Lady tried to stay clear of the partisan nonsense that surrounded her husband while in the Whitehouse. However, when her husband sought re-election in 2012 and was faced with a thought-provoking race against the Republican, Governor Mitt Romney, she toured the country and made public appearances in support of her husband's re-election campaign.

In October of 2016, the First Lady and Senator Clinton hit the campaign trail for the first time. Michelle Obama was able to utilize her widespread popularity and reputation for authenticity to help Senator Clinton. She also participated in a series of appearances in support of Hillary's campaign. The most extraordinary moment in the campaign was at the Democratic Convention when Michelle gave a ringing endorsement of Hillary Clinton that brought the supporters to tears. Senator Clinton appeared to tear up, as did many delegates when First Lady Obama compared Senator Clinton's potential to break the glass ceiling to President Obama's achievements as the first African-American president.

First Lady Michelle Obama Speech at Democratic National Convention

Brought Participates to Tears

*"The civil rights activists, delegates, and democrats of all
nationalities were wiping away tears."*

In my opinion, I have never heard a first lady give a speech so profound, thoughtful and well-articulated that almost everyone in the audience broke down into tears? First Lady Obama did. Michelle speech was intelligent, inspirational, thought-provoking and authentic. The best address ever heard during a Democratic National Convention? President

Obama, the first African American president of the United States, could only mouth "wow." The First Lady delivered the speech before delegates and ordinary democrats in Philadelphia Convention Center. Also, millions viewed the statement via television. When she brilliantly articulated her thoughts when she looked out the Whitehouse window and saw her two African-American children playing with their dog on the lawn of the house that slaves built, there wasn't a dry eye in the audience. The First Lady also referenced Senator Hillary Clinton statement about breaking the glass ceiling. Why, because if Senator Clinton won the election, she would be the first female President of the United States. First Lady Obama also disputed the naysayers who said a woman could never become president of the United States. At that moment, America was the greatest country in the world, because, for the first time in history, a woman had won the Democratic Party nomination for the President.

Historically Senator Hillary Rodman Clinton Was Not the First Women to Run for President of the United States

History tends to repeat itself. Did you know that Senator Hillary Rodman Clinton was not the first women to run or attempt to run for President of the United States of America? Senator Clinton, however, was the only women to be nominated by a major political party (Democratic Party) as an actual front-runner in a Presidential election. Historical record will show that Senator Clinton did win the popular votes. However, Donald Trump (now President Trump) won the electoral votes. Was Senator Hillary Rodman Clinton the only women to attempt the monumental task of running for President of the United States of America? No, she wasn't. Listed below are other women who ran for President. Unfortunately, many of them did not get as far as Senator Clinton.

Do You Know there were other *Women Who Ran for President?*

1. Victoria Claflin Woodhull (1872) earned the Equal Rights Party nominee during a period wherein women were not allowed to vote. Woodhull a suffragette believed that women should vote and had legal right to vote under the Privileges and Immunities Clause of the Constitution. She presented her argument before the House Judiciary Committee in 1871. However, the Supreme Court ruled against her. *Did you know that any female who showed up to vote in 1872 was arrested?*

2. Belva Ann Lockwood (1872) - the first woman to appear as a candidate on official ballots. She receives insults from many Newspapers during that period. She was called names, and the media said her election would lead to a feminism rule within the Whitehouse. Lockwood received approximately 4,000 votes. Also, some supporter's votes were missing. Belva attempted another run for president in 1888 which was unsuccessful.

3. Margaret-Chase Smith (1964) – ran opposite Barry Goldwater and won 37 out of 1, 308 convention vote. Even though she lost the primary election, she made headlines when she secured 25-percent of the votes in Illinois. She is well remembered for her 1950 speech, "Declaration of Conscience" wherein she questioned McCarthyism.

4. Shirley Chisholm (1972) - was the first African American woman elected to Congress in the United States. Chisholm, announced her bid for the presidency under the Democratic Party and took her campaign all the way to the DNC; like Senator Hillary Clinton. Shirley was one of the most practical political thinker during that era. Shirley said. "You can go to that Convention, and you can yell, 'Women power! Here I come!' You can yell, 'Black power! Here I come!' "The only thing those hard-nosed boys are going to understand is how many delegates you got". Hubert Humphrey released his black delegates to vote for Chisholm,

and she won 152 votes. Unfortunately, it wasn't enough to secure the nomination. However, she was able to address the crowd at the convention.

5. Patsy Matsu Takemoto Mink (1972) - a congresswoman from Hawaii who was a third-generation Japanese American and an anti-Vietnam War candidate. Ran on the Democratic ticket and received 2% of the votes. President Obama (2014) awarded her the Presidential Medal of Freedom for lifetime achievements.

6. Linda Jenness (1972) - ran for president on the Socialist Workers Party ticket. She was a socialist, and not seen as a serious candidate. However, she received over 80,000 votes in the '72 election. However, Linda 31 at the time and the legal age was 35 years old.

7. Geraldine Ferraro (1984) - New York congresswoman Geraldine Ferraro was chosen to be Senator Walter Mondale running mate. The first time a woman's name appears as the V.P. candidate on a major party ticket.

8. Pat Schroeder (1988) - a representative for Colorado when She gained the Democratic Party nomination for president after Gary Hart decided not to run. She enters the race for a short period. Schroeder press conference announcing her withdrawal from the campaign was referred to as "emotional" by the press. She was criticized for her emotional presentation and even received hate mail.

9. Elizabeth Dole (2000) - the wife of Republican Bob Dole, who was a U.S. Senate Majority Leader. Elizabeth graduated from Duke University with a BS in Political Science, Harvard University with an M.A Education and Harvard Law School with J.D. She was Secretary of Transportation for Ronald Regan and the Secretary of Labor for George H.W. Bush. Mrs. Dole was the Republican nominee in the 2000 presidential election. However, she dropped out of before the primaries.

10. Carol Moseley Braun (2004) - the first women elected to the Senate. She represented Illinois and the Democratic Party; in 2004 she ran for the Democratic Party's nomination. Braun wasn't successful at accumulating enough momentum. Because struggled with campaign funding, and she dropped out of the race just four days before the Iowa caucuses.

Popular Votes vs Electoral Votes of Presidents

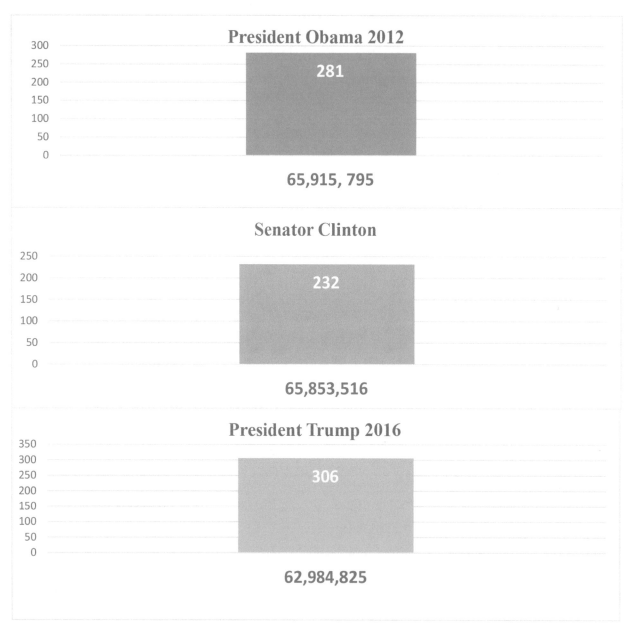

Statistical Data Source: Pew Research Center

The News Media Impact on the 2016 Campaign

Millions of Americans watched their favorite News Networks during the 2016 election campaign. Cable Networks like **BREITBART, FOX NEW, CNN,** and **MSNBC** viewership increased by millions, and the news outlet made millions of dollars through advertisements during the campaign and are still making millions covering President Trump.

BREITHART NEWS

Senator Clinton seemed to have a very cozy relationship with the mainstream media. However, an unforeseen News Network that impacted Hillary campaign was BREITBART NEWS, the Alt-Right News Network with over 240 million page views and 37 million unique visitors, who were mostly Donald Trump (President Trump) supporters. The pro-Donald Trump media narrative coming from Breitbart the extreme conservative, right-wing cable network dominated the news media with negative stories about Senator Clinton and her campaign. Steve Bannon, one of Donald Trump staunch supporters, is executive chairman of Breitbart News. Breitbart News Network spends hour after hour pandering to the far right fans of Donald Trump. They very aggressively and successfully promote negative stories and narratives about Senator Clinton, such as ex-president Bill Clinton's sexual scandals, Benghazi, and the Wikileaks email situation.

FOX NEWS

A News outlet that reported in favor of Donald Trump was FOX NEWS. Roger Ailes, the CEO, and the founder of Fox News supported Trump. Mr. Ailes put on his anti-Clinton gloves and went to work promoting Trump after being fired for allegedly sexually harassing some of Fox News female anchors.

FOX NEWS spent years denigrating President Obama as the source of America's problems. Donald Trump was a presidential candidate that rhetoric fits into Fox's traditional format. Fox supported a candidate who embellished the truth most of the time and quotes many unknowns as his sources. When he didn't have a legitimate source, he merely made it up, and Fox loved it. PolitiFact reported out of 158 statements made by the Republican candidate, Donald Trump, only four were rated as TRUE. Many conservatives get the majority of their news coverage from Fox News or conservative radio stations.

These conservatives tend to distrust all other news sources and refer to them as Fake News. However, Fox News anchors seemed apprehensive and embarrassed about the information Trump rendered. Even though, some of Fox News anchors didn't like Trump, Roger Ailes the CEO, and the founder of Fox News supported Trump. Mr. Ailes put on his anti-Clinton gloves and went to work supporting Trump after being fired for allegedly sexually harassing some of Fox News female anchors.

CNN

When it came to news coverage of Donald Trump and Hillary Clinton CNN tried to present itself as being unbiased. The strategy of CNN President Jeff Zucker was to place his people in front of candidates and carefully watched, expertly produced events that kept the CNN logo circulating throughout the campaign and way beyond.

MSNBC

MSNBC's strategy relied on positioning itself as a liberal alternative to FOX news and tried to be unbiased throughout their new coverages of the 2016 election. MSNBC was able to deliver reliable ratings during the 2016 campaign. It finished the month of August 2016 as the No. 2 cable news network in primetime viewers.

FAKE NEWS

"Yellow Journalism"

Did you know that Trump's first press conference as President-elect emphasized the term *"Fake News?"* However, this wasn't the first time the President referred to negative news about him or his campaign as Fake News. Since his election, the President has called out major media outlets several times a week for reporting Fake News via his Twitter feed. President Trump's arch enemies seem to be CNN, MSNBC, and the New York Times.

Internet and Fake News Society

If you want to experience the propaganda arms of FAKE NEWS, spend several hours on the Internet. With the invention of the Internet, came Fake News. Millions of Americans get most of their news from the Internet because it is quicker. Anyone can post information on the Internet. If individuals fail to read news reports carefully they may end up digesting mistruths and propaganda. Millions of people follow and believe everything they see or read via the Internet with very little time FACT CHECKING the information.

On the other hand, there are internet News Outlets that are well known for reporting accurate news via the internet and televisions. *See the list below*:

1. The Associate Press
2. C-Span
3. PBS
4. The Economist
5. Reuters
6. Snopes
7. NPR

8. BBC
9. New York Times
10. Wall Street Journal

Did you notice our President uses the **FAKE NEWS** narratives in many of his tweets? President Trump uses the term to describe news coverage that is supportive of his presidency or behavior. He mostly utilizes **FAKE NEWS NARRATIVE** when the news reports are accurate. Are you aware that the term **Fake News** was the Word of the Year in 2017?

"Social Media Revolution"

Did you know that social media usage was the beginning of constant information sharing between millions of people? The creation of social networks like Facebook, Google, Ingram, and Twitter allows millions of people to exchange information within mega seconds.

Web-based applications also allowed anyone to create a dynamic website to promote their business, books, and advertisement. Distribution and cost, because of Websites, save millions of dollars for corporations and small business. What has emerged because of the social media revolution is people have 24/7 to access to their friend, family, and various organizations.

The fallout from social media, unfortunately, is the very limited face-to-face interaction between social media junkies. Many people get all their information from social media outlets without considering the fact that some of the information is not accurate?

President Trump Tweeting Habits Appears to do More Harm than Good

"It's Raining Tweets"

President Trump's fighting back technique is through tweeting. *"His finger must be tired"*. Candidate Trump tweeted approximately 1,000 times during his campaign and 1800 times since his inauguration. He has generated a thunderstorm of tweets. Our President use tweeting as a method of beating back comments, situations, political and personal issues he believe is an affront to his presidency. President Trump also utilizes tweeting as a spin machine to send dog whistles to his support base. Hopefully, at some point our president will realize he is the president of all Americans, and his tweeting behavior will change. Hopefully, at this point, he will understand that the presidency is greater than he is.

The President also tweets negatively or mentions President Obama's name over and over again as though he is President Obama's Nemesis (long-standing rival; or archenemy). What is unprecedented about these tweets, they violated the unwritten protocol that every president before him had to respect. (This unwritten policy states that current presidents should not speak negatively about a former president. Nevertheless, President Trump has tweeted over and over again that his inauguration was more prominent than President Obama, which was not true. Did you know that President Trump spends countless hours tweeting about President Obama, and have compared himself to Obama's achievements approximately 1340 times? This behavior is bizarre and gives the American public the impression that he is jealous of his predecessors' political achievements.

President Trump does have the right to choose what he feels is essential to tweet. However, in 2017, he began tweeting about the African American players in the National Football League, as well as a player from the National Basketball League. Why, because the players decided to kneel and lock arms during the National Anthem in support for the Black Lives Matter Movement started by Collin Kaepernick and joined by Eric Reid during a 49ers football game. These players were protesting racial and social injustice against African-Americans.

The problem with reprimanding the NFL and NBA players was the President seemed to be unconcerned about the sports players' rights to exercise their 1st Amendment rights to protest. And there is no constitutional amendment associated with the pledge of allegiance. Nor is there a rule in the NFL handbook that mentions the National Anthem. However, unlike the NFL, the NBA has a policy/rule that states players must stand during the playing of the national anthem before all games. Did you know that standing and putting your hand over your heart during the National Anthem and Pledging Allegiance is a tradition?

The President's position was the National Anthem is representative of Americans patriotism. Even though many individuals supported the President speaking out, the situation escalated when President called the African American player "Sons of ----. This language outraged many Americans because his statement seen racist and divisive.

Some individuals felt President Trump made this an issue because national polls indicated that many Americans felt players who kneeled during the national anthem were disrespecting the sacrifices of the military. However, all the players who knelt down stated that they respect, love and supported the sacrifices of all military personnel.

President Trump just couldn't rejoice in the public support in September and October 2017. Even though the President was pleased with his political base and other support he did what some may refer to as a Trump' Move (a strategy that backfires on the President). President Trump encouraged Vice President (VP) Pence to attend a 49ers Colt game in his hometown of Indianapolis and instructed the VP to walk out if the player takes to their knees during the Anthem, which they did. It was common knowledge that the Commander-In-Chief was playing to his political base.

However, the media exposed the Vice President who used a private government jet to attend the game just to walk out. The episode drew scrutiny because it was a political stunt, which cost the taxpayer thousands.

The President sometimes means well. Unfortunately, he draws unnecessary criticism through his tweeting addiction and the way he uses language; which is not accidental. One of the criticisms during his one of his tweeting frenzy, was he, excessively tweeted about NFL/NBA protest, and very little time was spent tweeting about Hurricanes Maria apocalyptic devastation of Puerto Rico in 2017.

Did you know that Collin Kaepernick, who started the protest, lost his job? However, he gained respect and support from many football and basketball players, as well as many fans. Mr. Kaepernick in 2017 received the Gentlemen Quarterly (GQ) Citizen of the Year Award.

The President tweeted many times he did not believe in climate change, even though he is not a Climate Ecologist. He thinks the Paris Accord undermine our economy, and puts (the U.S.) at a permanent disadvantage. In fact, the Paris Agreement was founded upon the United Nations Framework Convention on Climate Change in March 1994. One hundred and ninety-seven (197) countries participate in the UNFCCC. It has "near-universal membership" across the globe. Also, the President has no legal obligation to stay in the PCA because it was never ratified by the Senate. On Thursday, June 1, 2017, President fulfilled one of his campaign promises and pulled the United States out of the Paris Climate Accord (PCA).

The President spends countless hours tweeting about Fake News. A possible reason is he does this is to manipulate his support base. The President may believe that many of the

News Reports, about him, are unfavorable and he wants to control the press coverages. President Trump started the Fake News narrative to manage support base perception of his presidency. In many cases, he uses twitters to embellish the truth using hyperboles (wherein the President repeats his words or statements over and over again). Our Commander-in-Chief has mastered the art of deception and intentional manipulation. The Fake News narrative has been used dictators, for decades to maintain power and control.

Donald Trump Coalition 2016 Winning Strategy

"Make America Great Again"

Did you know, "Let's Make America Great Again," originally was used by Ronald Reagan and George H.W. Bush in their campaigns? Mr. Trump maintains he did not know about MAGA until he ran for President. Nevertheless, Donald Trump use of MAGA created a lot of enthusiasm amongst poor, working class and some middle-class people in the rust belt of Americans. What is unknown is the fact that many of Trump's supporters are not racists. They were fed up with their economic conditions that were caused by the industrial decline and possible excessive regulation of the coal industry which cost these voters their jobs. Furthermore, the rise of opioid abuse hit white men hard in the Rust Belt states. If we take a trip down memory lane, many of same individuals were Democrats and voted the Democratic ticket in almost every election. What was under the political radar, the sheer amount of the low-income and working-class Americans, who felt disfranchised and were not enjoying the fruits of capitalism? Mr. Trump's campaign manager, Mrs. Kelly Ann Conway, who was extremely knowledgeable about people in the Rust Belt, encouraged Mr. Trump to constantly rally in these states, and because of her political savviness, put President Trump in the Whitehouse.

Many Americans who would like to believe all Whites who voted for President Trump were racists. Well the fact is, many of these individuals voted for President Obama in 2008 and 2012. Trump's coalition was merely successful in flipping the working poor and lower to -middle-class individuals that resulted in candidate Trump's going to the Whitehouse to begin his presidency.

Those Americans who believed President Trump manipulated the racist tendencies of some individuals' by utilizing racial idioms are probably right. Let's be real. There has been and still are politicians that use subtle race baiting while campaigning, Trump did it better and more successfully by turning traditional blue states to red. Trump gained 306 electoral votes and won the election. The rust belt states that helped Donald Trump win the election were Illinois, Indiana, Michigan, Ohio, and Pennsylvania.

The Drug Epidemic in American and Politics

"In 2015 the overdose deaths in America surpassed 50,000, due to abuse of heroin and prescription painkillers known as opioids."

All the candidates running during the primary election discussed their plans to end the drug epidemic. Research has shown that the drug addiction in American is at an all-time high, compared to other countries. According to the National Survey on Drug Use and Health (NSDUH), approximately 21.5 million American are addicted to alcohol and drugs. This addition affects people between the ages of 12 and older. What does this mean? One in every 10 Americans has substance abuse problems? Unfortunately, only 11 percent of those with an addiction problem get treatment.

The reason the 2016 candidates discussed the drug epidemic, was because of the use of illegal drugs drug in the United States had reached an unprecedented increase. Illicit drug

use has evolved from an inner city (i.e., black) crime to a suburban (i.e., white) disease. According to a 2015 Gallup poll of the use of "mood altering drugs" found that seven of the top 10 states had the highest level of abuse. The percent of those using the illegal drug, "almost every day," were red states located in the South, West Virginia (28.1%). These states included Kentucky (24.5%), Alabama (24.2%), Louisiana (22.9%), South Carolina (22.8%), Mississippi (22.3%) and Missouri (22.2%).
Illegal Drugs, Race and the 2016 Elections - Counterpunch.
http://www.counterpunch.org/2016/03/18/illegal-drugs-race-and-the-2016-elections/

The drug epidemic is the reason why Senator Clinton and Senator Sanders throughout the campaign, discussed a plan that would include rehabilitation and treatment vs. prison. While on the other hand, Senator Cruz and Donald Trump called for treatment, prevention and securing the United States border to disrupt the drug trafficking associated with the Mexican border.

The Political War against Drug

"Drugs, Drugs and More Drugs=Death"

There is a long history of the abuse of opioids, including prescription painkillers and heroin in the United States. There are millions of Americans addictive to opiates and heroin in America. October of 2017 our President declared the opioid crises a national public health emergency. Will our President allocate funding to aid epidemic relief organizations and educate the public on drug prevention? If not, the next question becomes WHY NOT?

Reality Television Impact on the 2016 Election

"What were they thinking or were they thinking?"

Did you know an estimated 84 million people watched the news for hours? Why, because this was the first time in history that a presidential campaign presented itself in a Reality

TV format? The campaign of 2016 had name calling, joking about a news reporter with a disability, mistruths, a sex video, outraging behavior and controversial situations on a daily basis. It was although people felt the election campaign was electrifying and fascinating. The same attitude millions of American had towards reality shows were transformed to the 2016 campaign. Donald Trump, known for his reality TV show, "The Apprentice" stating, "You're Fired!" He ran his campaign the same way. Mr. Trump, who was unknown on political radar was the "appealing plot line" and won the 2016 election using a reality TV format. It was has through people forgot they were electing a President; who is the head of government of the United States and referred to as Commander-in-Chief. Also, it seemed as though they were ambiguous to the fact that the President signs executive orders and legislative agendas that affect millions of Americans on a daily basis.

One has to contemplate whether some voters were so entertained by the drama and became so immune to the behavior of candidates during the election that they didn't vote or voted against their own economic and social interest.

Social Media Platforms Impact on the Election of 2016

"In the 21ˢᵗ century millions of people live in cyberspace"

Social media platforms are where people interface with each other in seconds. Individual and companies generate large support using these platforms every day. They utilize social media to advertise, sell products, communicates with friends and family, inform others of all types of events and just information sharing, and this is done all over the throughout the world. Millions of people spend countless hours in cyberspace so it wasn't difficult to understand how these "social media platforms" could play a pivotal role in the election. You can reach people 24/7 through mobile devices (cell phones), non-calling tablets that comes with Wi-Fi support, tablets that connect to 4G cellular wireless networks and of course you can access social media through computers-- regardless of where they are. President Obama was extremely social-media-savvy and utilized social media successfully to become the 1st African American President in 2008 and reelected in 2012.

Senator Clinton and Donald Trump connected to millions of voters, especially the millenniums, through Facebook, Twitter, YouTube and Instagram because it takes seconds to upload images, text messages, and video to these sites. When the candidates utilized any of these social media platforms, they were able to generate followers, and these followers were able to forward these items to their friends, which give the candidates access to other supporters. Eventually, the candidates accumulated millions of supporters, which translated into votes. The candidates also used social media to raise millions in campaign donations with little or no cost to them.

"While everyone else was sleeping, Donald Trump was Tweeting".

Senator Clinton and Mr. Trump both used social media extensively throughout their campaigns and a strong presence on Twitter. In addition, the attention they received from the public on Facebook and other outlets was prevalent throughout the campaign. Clinton used links to highlight official campaign communications while Trump frequently related his posts to the news media. Trump retweeted people more often than Clinton. Clinton used videos that appeared in about a quarter of Clinton's social media posts, compared with about one tenth of Trump's posts. Nevertheless, on all of the platforms both candidates mentioned their opponents and Mr. Trump used Twitter like there was no tomorrow (tweeting 24/7).

Instagram also played a significant role for both candidates, especially Mr. Trump, because he instantly uploaded all of his rallies that included derogatory statements about Senator Hillary and President Obama. Some folks believed that social media was the fuel for the vehicle that drove President Trump to the White House.

"Social Media Played a Historic Role in the 2016 Elections".

Trump's success with social media gained him approximately 22.7 million likes and followers on Facebook, Twitter, and Instagram. While on the other hand, Clinton only accumulated 15 million views on Facebook, Twitter, and Instagram. Nonetheless, Senator Clinton was far ahead when it came to YouTube videos. Her political advertisement helped her gain appropriately 16.4 million views compared to Trump's 8.1 million views.
Fact Check checked via several mediums.

Social Media and News Organizations

Facebook users tended to interact with articles from FOX and CNN. By far the source with the most associated articles was FOX, CNN, and BREITBART who were neck-and-neck with more than 18 million interactions. Given the dozen of news network on the left, CNN, ABC, NBC, MSNBC generally differed in assumptions and behavior.

News Papers Who support Senator Clinton vs Candidate Trump

Hillary seemed to be the daring of the hardcopy print media. Apparently, hardcopy media outlets were competing with social media outlets and print media competed with social media. But people have to understand that print media was trying to increase sales in an era where most individuals receive daily doses of news via Social Media. The average cost of newspaper in 2016 was 75c to $1.00. Approximately, 39 hard copy media outlets across the county printed articles that endorsed Senator Clinton while only ten newspapers publishers, supported candidate Trump.

President Trump's Economic Theory

"Trickle-Down Economics"

JOBS OPPORUNITIES MAYBE?

If 2/3 of President Trump' cabinet have the net worth equal to 1/3 of the American population (approximately 100 million people), it appears that the president adheres to the trickle-down theory of economics. Trickle-down economics is a theory that advocates benefits for the wealthy, trickle down to the unemployed, working class and middle-class citizens of America. The premise of this belief is based on the theory that if you give tax cuts to millionaires and billionaires business owners, this will encourage various business organizations to expand and create more jobs.

This theory assumes in the simplest terms that investors, savers and company owners are the real drivers of the economic growth of the economy. It also assumes financial institutions like banks will increase lending to businesses. Owners of these company and business organizations will invest, expand their operations and hire more workers; the workers will spend their wages on many more goods and services, therefore increasing economic growth. The republican 2017 tax plans is an example of the "Trickle-down" theory.

"Trickle-Up Economics"

The "Trickle-up" theory is referred to as the Keynes theory of economics. The "Trickle-up" economics theorists believe that if you lower taxes and other economic burdens on the upper and middle class, they will invest in education for the working class and underprivileged, these folks can get better jobs in a technology-enhanced society. People should be able to obtain suitable employment and create a stronger workforce. Also, the theory adheres to the concept that this increases wealth creation in the United States. One of the principle components of this theory is working Americans will purchase more goods and services and the profit will "Trickle-up" to the wealthiest members of society which will ultimately lead to business expansion and improve public service in America.

If more people are working and saving, banks will lower interest rates and make funds available to entrepreneurs. Individuals who organize and operate businesses will be able to generate more jobs and opportunities for others in America as well as create a financially healthy society.

The Impact of Cyberwarfare and the 2016 Election

Cyberwarfare is the use of computer technology to disrupt the activities of a state or organization, especially the deliberate attacking of information systems for strategic or military purposes. In cyber warfare, hackers are professional computer programmers who write computer programming codes to access someone else computer server. The purpose is to steal valuable information saved on the server. In many cases, hackers sell or distribute information to other corporations or countries. ****For individuals who are not computer savvy, a hacker is a thief, who survey your home, come up with ways to bypass your home security system, locate your valuable, steal them and sell them to someone else.****

Hackers can access a company or personal data from a local area network (LAN) or wide area network (WAN) via the internet. Microsoft Cloud is referred to as "cloud computer" meaning everywhere. Cloud computing allows individuals to store and access their data and programs over the web instead of your computer's hard drive. The term Cloud means the Internet. This information can also be accessed from your mobile device.

Senator Clinton was using a private server at her home when her emails were hacked and were supposedly leaked by Wikileaks. The hackers also hacked into the Democratic National Committee (DNC) server as well.

Julian Assange, the founder of Wikileaks leaked Senator Clinton and the DNC emails. What agitated the Clinton campaign was Donald Trump's request for Wikileaks to release more of Senator Clinton's email during his campaign rallies. The Democrats and other non-supporters of Senator Clinton believed that Donald Trump benefited from Wikileaks email release. Americans were paying attention to the Wikileaks releases of the Senator emails, even though there was a lot of nonsense taken place in the final weeks of both campaigns. However, many voters believed that Wikileaks' email scandal did impede Senator Clinton election result to some degree.

Brief History of President Putin

One cannot speak about a Russian Connection without knowing a brief history of the Prime Minister of Russia. Vladimir Putin graduated from one of the most prestigious colleges in Leningrad. Putin, if you didn't know, is a lawyer. Also, Vladimir Putin was an intelligence officer of the KBG, before becoming the Prime Minister of the Russia in 1999. In 2008, after handing the presidency over to Medvedev; V was appointed Prime Minister of Russia, and in September 2011, when the term limit became six years, Putin pursued a third term as president.

President Putin is a person who responded to changes quickly when confronted with unpredictable circumstances. It appears Putin has mastered the role of being a people puppeteer and enjoys manipulating individuals whom he perceives as narcissistic, grandiose and self-centered. Putin seems to understand people who are willing to do anything to maintain a sit of power. Therefore, he has become a master at playing people like a violin. The question becomes, is President Trump one of the people he seems to enjoy *playing like a violin?*

The Russian Scandal That Engulfed President Trump's White House

"Members of the House and Senate believe the Russian did interfere in 2016 election through the use of Cyberwarfare".

The problem with the Trump's Whitehouse is the peculiar relationship between President Trump and President Putin. The Russian connection is different from other scandals that have plagued presidents in the past. Why? Because it involves a foreign power possible interfering with a United States election. Even though the United States' intelligence agencies concluded that Russia interfered in the election. President Trump played down the involvement. Some Americans believe Russians interfered with the election but do not think the inferenced the 2016 election outcome. On the other hand, Americans are not sure whether Russian is a friend or foe. If Russians did interfere, what did they want?

The 2016 election was different because it involved hacking and cyber warfare. In September of 2017, it was discovered that agents of the Russia government placed Black Lives Matter Ads on Facebook targeting Baltimore and Ferguson. Also, trolls, (suspected Russian agents) purchased the advertisement on Twitters, Google, and Facebook. The Russian scandal plagued the Trump Whitehouse. The majority of congressional members believe there are some serious issues when it comes to the Russians intervening in the United States election process.

Presidential Scandals

"The strength of a nation derives from the integrity of the house."

By: Confucius

Did you know that scandals are nothing new to the White House or the Presidency? President Trumps' White House Russian scandal will be part of the dynamic and unnecessary trauma historians will write about in the future. Past scandals include: Andrew Jackson, Ulysses S. Grant's, James Garfield, Grover Cleveland, Warren G. Harding, Richard Nixon, Ronald Reagan, and of course William (Bill) Clinton.

Andrew Jackson married a woman, Rachel Donelson in 1791. The married wasn't legal because Rachel wasn't divorced from her previous husband. Rachel ex-husband was supposed to get the divorce, and for some odd reason, he didn't. When this information reached the public, it impacted Andrew Jackson run for office in 1828. However, he was able to overcome the scandal and became the 7th President of the United States in 1829.

Ulysses S. Grant's presidency was scandal central. The scandals included the Gold Market, Credit Mobilier Company, and the Whiskey Rings Scandals in 1875, and *James Garfield*, had to deal the Star Route Scandal in 1881, six months before being assassinated. His interception dealt with corruption in the postal service, which was handled by private organizations.

Grover Cleveland, scandal took place in 1884, while he was campaigning for president. Glover who had an affair with a widower named Maria C. Halpin who gave birth to his son, Oscar Folsom Cleveland. Cleveland did the honorable thing financially supporting Oscar, and paying to put Oscar in an orphanage when Maria couldn't take care of him. Cleveland, a Democrat, won the presidential election in 1888, many people believed it was because of the way he treated Maria, C. Halpin and *Warren G. Harding's* presidency involved the Teapot Dome scandal-- also referred to as the Elk Hills Scandal from 1921 to 1922.

Richard Nixon, Watergate was the name given to the presidential scandal in 1972. Many Americans still remember this incident. Five men were caught breaking into the Democratic National Headquarters located at the Watergate business complex. Nixon was almost impeached for this incident. However, he resigned on August 9, 1974. A good depiction of what happen can be seen in "All the President's Men" a 1976 film about the Watergate scandal

Ronald Reagan, scandal was Iran-Contra Scandal. Individuals in Ronald Reagan's obtained money through selling arms to Iran secretly to the revolutionary Contras in Nicaragua. Along with helping the Contras, the hope was that by selling the weapons to Iran, terrorists would be more willing to give up hostages. This scandal resulted in major Congressional hearings.

William, (Bill) Clinton, Achilles heel was the Monica Lewinsky affair. Lewinsky was a White House staffer whom Clinton had a sexual affair for over a year. After nearly 14 hours of debate, the House of Representatives approved two articles of impeachment, charging him with lying under oath to a federal grand jury and obstructing justice. He tried to deny the affairs while giving a deposition in another case; which resulted in a vote to impeach him by the House of Representatives in 1998.

Russian Scandal

"How does the Russian scandal fits into the America political landscape?"

"What Going On..."

President Trump's decision to fire FBI James Comey generated new questions about an investigation into the Russian connection during the 2016 campaign, resulted in the former FBI Director Mueller being appointed as Special Counsel to investigate Russian connection. Because this is still an open investigation, the authors of this book decline to comment on the subject.

Russia, Iran and North Korea Sanctions

"When it rains, it pours" (English Proverb)

Senate and the House of Representatives passed sweeping sanctions bill against **Russia**, **Iran** and **North Korea** with an overwhelming bipartisan majority, 97-2. The House voted 419-3 to pass the sanction bills. On August 2, 2017 President Trump signed H.R. 3364 - Countering America's Adversaries through Sanctions Act-To continue the sanctions placed on Russia, Iran and North Korean.

"Russia's Sanctions in 2014"

The United States sanctioned Russia was because of the Russian annexation of the Crimea from Ukraine. Russian citizens were subject to travel bans, and frozen assets. Russian companies became restricted in their activities in the United States and Europe. These individuals were a part of Russia's powerful elite, and members of President Vladimir Putin's inner circle. The sanctions aimed at hurting the Russian economy. On December 29, US President Barack Obama announced additional sanctions because of allegations the Russia interfered in the 2016 election.

"Iran Sanctions in 1979"

In November 1979, the United States imposed sanctions against after Iranian students who invaded the US embassy and captured American diplomats and held them as hostages. Iranian products were banned and could not be imported into the United States except for small gifts, information material, foodstuffs and some carpets. Iranian assets were also frozen, October 2012, Iran's currency fell to a new record low and economists contributed the fall as a direct result of international pressure.

The European Union tightened their sanctions on the country's banking, trade, and energy sectors prohibiting any transactions with Iranian banks, as well as sanctions on Iranian natural gas.

"North Korea Sanctions in 1985"

North Korea links other issues to this provision of the treaty including the withdrawal of U.S. nuclear weapons from South Korea. For years, the United States and the international community have tried to negotiate an end to North Korea's nuclear and missile development and its export of ballistic missile technology. Those efforts have been replete with periods of crisis, stalemate, and tentative progress towards eliminating nuclear weapons. North Korea has long been a key challenge for the global nuclear nonproliferation regime.

The United States has pursued a variety of policy responses to the proliferation challenges posed by North Korea, including military cooperation with U.S. allies in the region, wide-ranging sanctions, and non-proliferation mechanisms such as export controls. The United States also engaged in two major diplomatic initiatives to have North Korea abandon its nuclear weapons efforts in return for aid.

In 1994, faced with North Korea's announced intent to withdraw from the nuclear Nonproliferation Treaty (NPT), which requires non-nuclear weapon states to forswear the development and acquisition of nuclear weapons, the United States and North Korea signed it. Pyongyang committed to freezing its illicit plutonium weapons program in exchange for aid.

Following the collapse of this agreement in 2002, North Korea claimed that it had withdrawn from the NPT in January 2003 and once again began operating its nuclear facilities.

The second major diplomatic effort were the Six-Party Talks initiated in August of 2003 which involved China, Japan, North Korea, Russia, South Korea, and the United States. In between periods of stalemate and crisis, those talks arrived at critical breakthroughs in 2005, when North Korea pledged to abandon "all nuclear weapons and existing nuclear programs" and return to the NPT, and in 2007, when the parties agreed on a series of steps to implement that 2005 agreement.

Those talks, however, broke down in 2009 following disagreements over verification and an internationally condemned North Korea rocket launch. Pyongyang has since stated that it would never return to the talks and is no longer bound by their agreements. The other five parties state that they remain committed to the talks, and have called for Pyongyang to recommit to its 2005 denuclearization pledge.

The following chronology summarizes in greater detail developments in North Korea's nuclear and missile programs, and the efforts to end them, since 1985 to the 2017.

*Did you know there were four U.S. Presidents who politically tried
to deal with North Korean prior to President Trump?*

President Ronald Reagan, George Bush, Jr., William Clinton, and Barrack Obama: has to deal with North Korea. Now it time for President Trump to understanding what these presidents were face with. Now it is. President Trump turn to deal with North Korean, Supreme Leader; Kim Jong-un. Listed below are all the dates the United States had to deal with North Korean.

The readers can review the detail information via the dates listed below:

1985, 1991, 1992, 1993, 1994, 1995, 1996, 1997, 1998, 1999, 2000, 2001, 2002, 2003,2004,2005,2006 2007, 2008, 2009, 2010, 2011, 2012, 2013, 2014, 2015, 2016, 2017

* Entry dates for the imposition of sanctions indicate the dates the sanctions took effect.
https://www.armscontrol.org/factsheets/dprkchron#1985

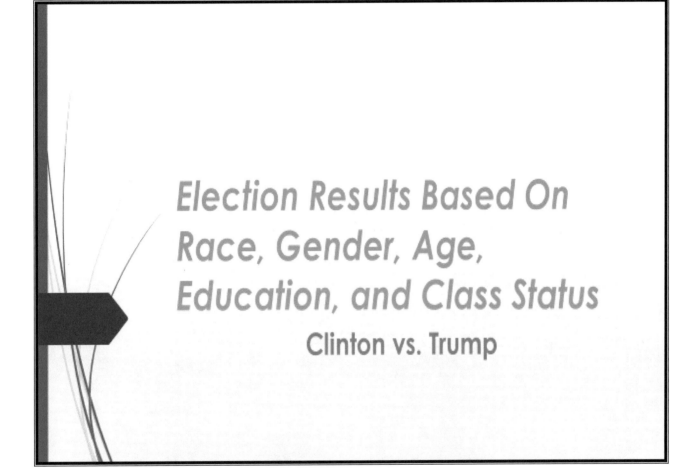

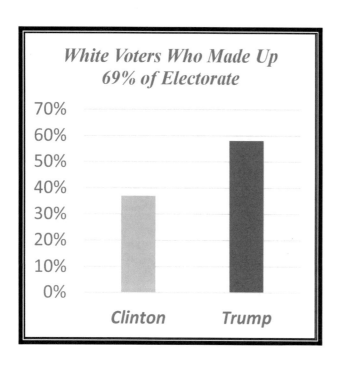

White Voters Who Made Up 69% of Electorate

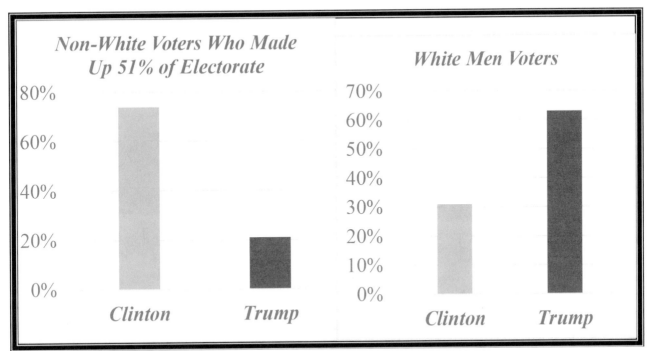

Non-White Voters Who Made Up 51% of Electorate

Clinton · Trump

White Men Voters

Clinton · Trump

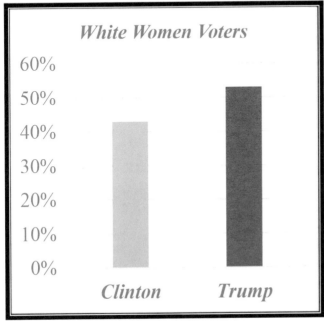

White Women Voters

Clinton · Trump

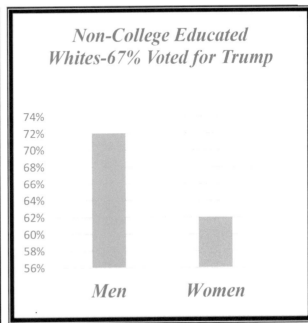

Non-College Educated Whites-67% Voted for Trump

Men · Women

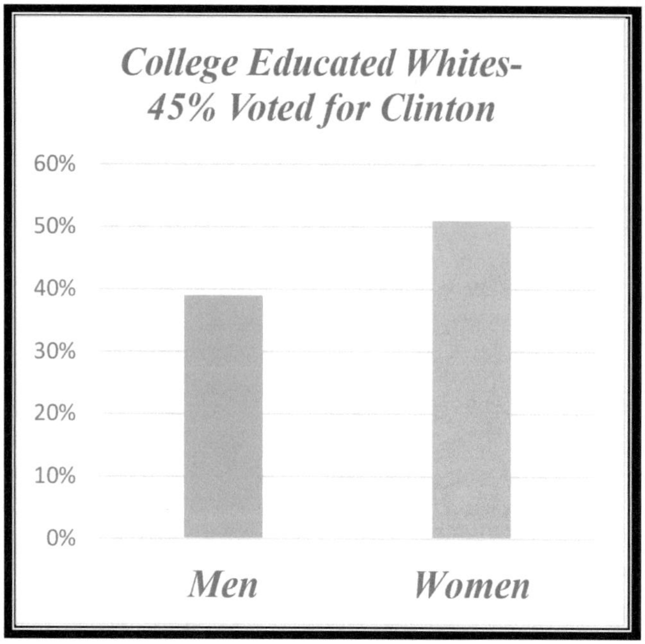
College Educated Whites-
45% Voted for Clinton
60%
50%
40%
30%
20%
10%
0%
Men
Women

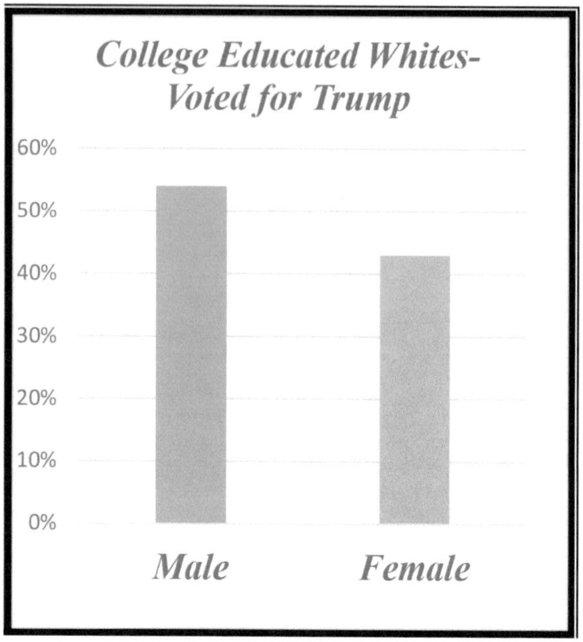
College Educated Whites-
Voted for Trump
60%
50%
40%
30%
20%
10%
0%
Male
Female

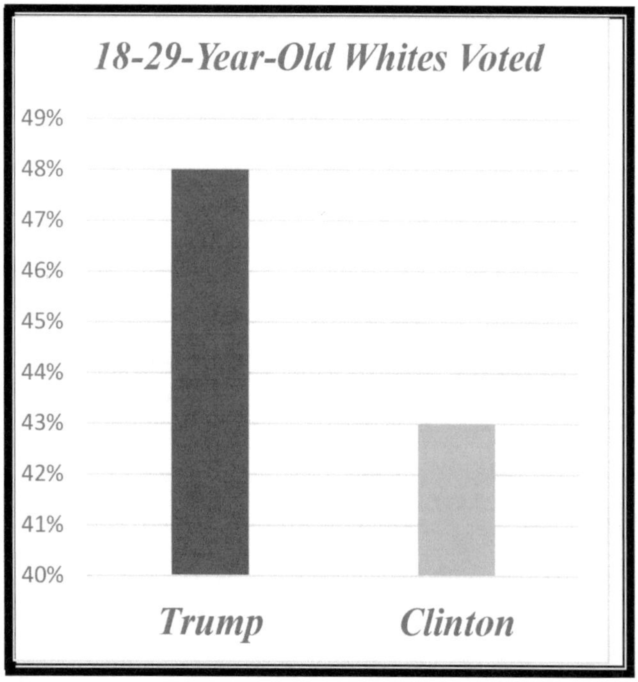
18-29-Year-Old Whites Voted
49%
48%
47%
46%
45%
44%
43%
42%
41%
40%
Trump
Clinton

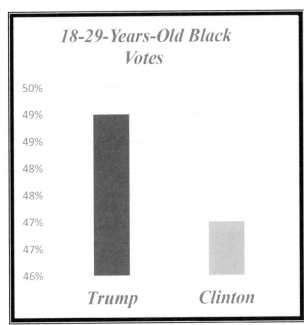

18-29-Years-Old Black Votes

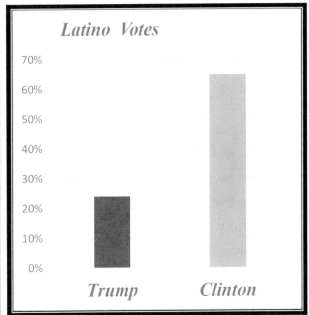

Latino Votes

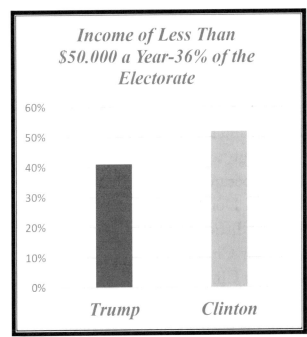

Income of Less Than $50.000 a Year-36% of the Electorate

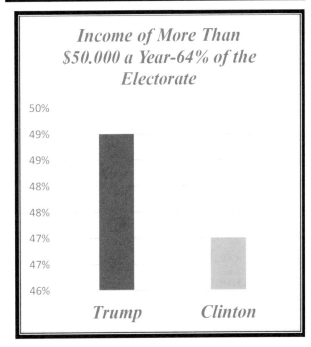

Income of More Than $50.000 a Year-64% of the Electorate

Pew Research Center

Has the Democrats Lost Their Mojo?

The Democratic National Committee seemed to have lost their mojo. In other words there are major problems with organizational objectives or either a sound strategy for getting Democrats elected to office in 2017. In a recent high-stakes special election for a Georgia House of Representative, Karen Handel defeated Democrat Jon Ossoff. Even though, the Democrat spent a millions on the race, making this election the most expensive House race in ever. Many candidates and outside organizations ended up spending over %55 million in the battle for the Republican-held district in Atlanta. Representative Handel successful win helps the Republicans maintain control of the House of Representatives. This election campaign was the most expensive campaign ever recorded in history.

Do Politicians Embellish the Truth?

"Liar! Liar! Pants on Fire!"?

It's widely known that many politicians lie. Even, some people tell untruth from time to time. However, Americans understand that excessive political lying is a strategy used by the politician to divert the voters' attention from the truth and facts. Nevertheless, in the 2016 campaign, both candidates lied throughout the campaign, and many voters were frustrated because at some point they were crossing the line. It became unbelievable the number of lies the candidates told each day. Senator Clinton and Donald Trump may not have had much in common; they share lying. Many people had difficulty believing what they were saying and couldn't keep up with all the lies. Senator Clinton and Donald Trump lied numerous times. During the debates between Senator Clinton and Donald Trump; they told at least 137 lies over the three presidential debates. Excluding, the many falsehoods Mr. Trump spews daily on the campaign trail; roughly one lie every 50 seconds.

Can the President Govern by Executive Orders Only?

The answer is probably no because the United States is a Republic, and the document used to help maintain an equal balance of power is the Constitution, which has three primary functions. First, our government consists of legislative, executive, and judicial branches. Second, there is a system of checks and balances among the three branches. Third, the constitution divides power between the federal government and the states.

Were you aware that Presidents can only utilize executive orders to push their political agenda? Why, because the U.S. Supreme Court held states that the Constitution has to support executive orders. Also, Congress must uphold some executive orders through the delegation of power to the President.

Did you know that Executive orders are issued by United States Presidents and directed towards officers and agencies of the United States? These orders are laws based on the authority derived from statutes or the Constitution. All Presidents sign into law executive orders to keep some of their campaign promises. Listed below is a list of executive orders and the dates that President Trump signed then into law.

President Trump Executives Orders

President Trump has signed 119 Executive Orders-Listed below are 61. See if you can locate the any of the 61 that will have a direct impact on your life. Additional Executive Orders can be viewed on: https://www.whitehouse.gov/briefing-room/presidential-actions

Executive Order on January 20, 2017

Executive Order Minimizing the Economic Burden of the Patient Protection Affordable Care Act Pending Repeal

1. **Executive Order** on January 24, 2017

   Executive Order Expediting Environmental Reviews and Approvals for High Priority Infrastructure Projects

2. **Executive Order** on January 25, 2017

   Executive Order: Enhancing Public Safety in the Interior of the United States

3. **Executive Order** on January 25, 2017

   Executive Order: Border Security and Immigration Enforcement Improvements

4. **Executive Order** on January 27, 2017

   Executive Order: Protecting the Nation from Foreign Terrorist Entry into the United States

5. **Executive Order** on January 28, 2017

   Executive Order: Ethics Commitments by Executive Branch Appointees

6. **Executive Order** on January 30, 2017

   Presidential Executive Order on Reducing Regulation and Controlling Regulatory Costs

7. **Executive Order** on February 03, 2017

   Presidential Executive Order on Core Principles for Regulating the United States Financial System

8. **Executive Order** on February 09, 2017

   Presidential Executive Order on Preventing Violence against Federal, State, Tribal, and Local Law Enforcement Officers

9. **Executive Order** on February 09, 2017

   Presidential Executive Order on a Task Force on Crime Reduction and Public Safety

10. **Executive Order** on February 09, 2017

    Presidential Executive Order on Enforcing Federal Law with Respect to Transnational Criminal Organizations and Preventing International Trafficking

11. **Executive Order** on February 09, 2017

    Providing an Order of Succession within the Department of Justice

12. **Executive Order** on February 24, 2017

    Presidential Executive Order on Enforcing the Regulatory Reform Agenda

13. **Executive Order** on February 28, 2017

    Presidential Executive Order on Restoring the Rule of Law, Federalism, and Economic Growth by Reviewing the "Waters of the United States" Rule

14. **Executive Order** on February 28, 2017

    Presidential Executive Order on the White House Initiative to Promote Excellence and Innovation at Historically Black Colleges and Universities

15. **Executive Order** on March 06, 2017

    Executive Order Protecting the Nation from Foreign Terrorist Entry into the United States

16. **Executive Order** on March 13, 2017

    Presidential Executive Order on a Comprehensive Plan for Reorganizing the Executive Branch

17. **Executive Order** on March 27, 2017

    Presidential Executive Order on the Revocation of Federal Contracting Executive Orders

18. **Executive Order** on March 28, 2017

    Presidential Executive Order on Promoting Energy Independence and Economic Growth

19. **Executive Order** on March 29, 2017

    Presidential Executive Order Establishing the President's Commission on Combating Drug Addiction and the Opioid Crisis

20. **Executive Order** on March 31, 2017

    Presidential Executive Order Regarding the Omnibus Report on Significant Trade Deficits

21. **Executive Order** on March 31, 2017

    Presidential Executive Order on Providing an Order of Succession within the Department of Justice

22. **Executive Order** on March 31, 2017

    Presidential Executive Order on Establishing Enhanced Collection and Enforcement of Antidumping and Countervailing Duties and Violations of Trade and Customs Laws

23. **Executive Order** on April 18, 2017

    Presidential Executive Order on Buy American and Hire American

24. **Executive Order** on April 21, 2017

    Presidential Executive Order on Identifying and Reducing Tax Regulatory Burdens

25. **Executive Order** on April 25, 2017

    Presidential Executive Order on Promoting Agriculture and Rural Prosperity in America

26. **Executive Order** on April 26, 2017

    Presidential Executive Order on the Review of Designations under the Antiquities Act

27. **Executive Order** on April 26, 2017

    Presidential Executive Order on Enforcing Statutory Prohibitions on Federal Control of Education

28. **Executive Order** on April 27, 2017
    Presidential Executive Order on Improving Accountability and Whistleblower Protection at the Department of Veterans Affairs

29. **Executive Order** on April 28, 2017
    Presidential Executive Order Implementing an America-First Offshore Energy Strategy

30. **Executive Order** on April 29, 2017
    Presidential Executive Order on Establishment of Office of Trade and Manufacturing Policy

31. **Executive Order** on April 29, 2017
    Presidential Executive Order Addressing Trade Agreement Violations and Abuses

32. **Executive Order** on May 01, 2017
    Presidential Executive Order on the Establishment of the American Technology Council

33. **Executive Order** on May 04, 2017
    Presidential Executive Order Promoting Free Speech and Religious Liberty

34. **Executive Order** on May 11, 2017
    Presidential Executive Order on Strengthening the Cybersecurity of Federal Networks and Critical Infrastructure

35. **Executive Order** on May 11, 2017
    Presidential Executive Order on the Establishment of Presidential Advisory Commission on Election Integrity

36. **Executive Order** on June 15, 2017
   Presidential Executive Order Expanding Apprenticeships in America

37. **Executive Order** on June 21, 2017
   Presidential Executive Order Amending Executive Order 13597

38. **Executive Order** on June 30, 2017
   Presidential Executive Order on Reviving the National Space Council

39. **Executive Order** on July 11, 2017
   Presidential Executive Order on Allowing Additional Time for Recognizing Positive Actions by the Government of Sudan and Amending Executive Order 13761

40. **Executive Order** on July 19, 2017
   Presidential Executive Order Establishing a Presidential Advisory Council on Infrastructure

41. **Executive Order** on August 15, 2017
   Presidential Executive Order on Establishing Discipline and Accountability in the Environmental Review and Permitting Process for Infrastructure

42. **Executive Order** on August 25, 2017
   Presidential Executive Order on Imposing Sanctions with Respect to the Situation in Venezuela

43. **Executive Order** on August 28, 2017
   Presidential Executive Order on Restoring State, Tribal, and Local Law Enforcement›s Access to Life-Saving Equipment and Resources

44. **Executive Order** on September 13, 2017
Order Regarding the Proposed Acquisition of Lattice Semiconductor Corporation by China Venture Capital Fund Corporation Limited

45. **Executive Order** on September 21, 2017
Presidential Executive Order on Imposing Additional Sanctions with Respect to North Korea

46. **Executive Order** on September 29, 2017
Presidential Executive Order on the Continuance of Certain Federal Advisory Committees

47. **Executive Order** on September 29, 2017
Presidential Executive Order on the Revocation of Executive Order Creating Labor-Management Forums

48. **Executive Order** on October 12, 2017
Presidential Executive Order Promoting Healthcare Choice and Competition Across the United States

49. **Executive Order** on October 20, 2017
Presidential Executive Order Amending Executive Order 13223

50. **Executive Order** on October 24, 2017
Presidential Executive Order on Resuming the United States Refugee Admissions Program with Enhanced Vetting Capabilities

51. November 28, 2017
Bernie Marcus: "GOP should unite for legacy tax-reform vote"

52. **Executive Order** on November 28, 2017

Statement from the Press Secretary on the Tax Cuts and Jobs Act Passing the Senate Budget Committee

53. **Executive Order** on November 28, 2017

The Wall Street Journal: "America's New Energy Diplomacy"

54. **Executive Order** on November 28, 2017

Investor's Business Daily: "The Latest Tax Cut Lie: The Senate Bill Will Hurt The Poor"

55. **Executive Order** on November 27, 2017

"Sen. Rand Paul: Here's why I plan to vote for the Senate tax bill..."

56. **Executive Order** on November 27, 2017

Readout of President Donald J. Trump's Call with President Emmanuel Macron of France

57. **Executive Order** on November 27, 2017

Economists: "How Tax Reform Will Lift the Economy"

58. **Executive Order** November 27, 2017

Statement from President Donald J. Trump on #GivingTuesday

59. **Executive Order** November 27, 2017

White House Statement on Director Mulvaney's Status as Acting Director of the Consumer Financial Protection Bureau

60. **Executive Order** November 27, 2017

Readout of the Vice President's Meeting with his Majesty King Abdullah II

Legislation and Congress in 2017

Did you know that legislation is a law or bill that is voted on by the Legislative Branch of government? The legislative branch has two components, the Senate and the House of Representatives. Once this bill or law gets a majority vote, it is then passed on to the president for approval, if the bill or law is approved it is then signed by the president. See if you see legislation that directly relates to your life. If you would like to view more legislation passed in 2017 go to:

https://www.whitehouse.gov/briefing-room/
signed-legislation?field_legislation_status_value=0&page=1

Legislation

1. **Signed** on September 14, 2017
    S.J.Res. 49 - Joint Resolution condemning the violence and domestic terrorist attack that took place during events between August 11 and August 12, 2017, in Charlottesville, Virginia, recognizing the first responders who lost their lives...

2. **Signed** on September 12, 2017
    H.R. 3732 - Emergency Aid to American Survivors of Hurricanes Irma and Jose Overseas Act

3. **Signed** on September 11, 2017
    S. 1616 - Bob Dole Congressional Gold Medal Act

4. **Signed** on September 8, 2017
    H.R. 601 - Continuing Appropriations Act, 2018 and Supplemental Appropriations for Disaster Relief Requirements Act, 2017

5. **Signed** on August 23, 2017
    H.R.2288 - Veterans Appeals Improvement and Modernization Act of 2017

6. **Signed** on August 22, 2017
    H.R. 339 - An Act to amend Public Law 94–241 with respect to the Northern Mariana Islands.

7. **Signed** on August 22, 2017
    H.J.Res.76 - Joint Resolution granting the consent and approval of Congress for the Commonwealth of Virginia, the State of Maryland, and the District of Columbia to a enter into a compact relating to the establishment of the Washington Metrorail.

8. **Signed** on August 18, 2017
    H.R. 873 - Global War on Terrorism War Memorial Act

9. **Signed** on August 18, 2017
    H.R. 510 - Rapid DNA Act of 2017

10. **Signed** on August 18, 2017
    H.R. 374 - An Act to remove the sunset provision of section 203 of Public Law 105–384, and for other purposes

11. **Signed** on August 4, 2017
    H.R. 3298 - Wounded Officers Recovery Act, 2017

12. **Signed** on August 2, 2017
    H.R. 3364 - Countering America's Adversaries through Sanctions Act

13. **Signed** on June 30, 2017
    H.R. 1238 - Securing our Agriculture and Food Act

14. **Signed** on June 27, 2017
    S. 1083 - An Act to amend section 1214 of title 5, United States Code, to provide for stays during a period that the Merit Systems Protection Board lacks a quorum

15. **Signed** on June 23, 2017
    S. 1094 - Department of Veterans Affairs Accountability and Whistleblower Protection Act of 2017

16. **Signed** on June 14, 2017
    H.R. 657 - Follow the Rules Act

17. **Signed** on June 6, 2017
    H.R. 375 - An Act to designate the Federal building and United States courthouse located at 719 Church Street in Nashville, Tennessee, as the "Fred D. Thompson Federal Building and United States Courthouse".

18. **Signed** on June 6, 2017
    H.R. 366 - DHS Stop Asset and Vehicle Excess Act or the DHS SAVE Act

19. **Signed** on June 2, 2017
    S. 583 - American Law Enforcement Heroes Act of 2017

20. **Signed** on June 2, 2017
    S. 419 - Public Safety Officers' Benefits Improvement Act of 2017

21. **Signed** on May 17, 2017

    H.J. Res. 66 - Joint Resolution disapproving the rule submitted by the Department of Labor relating to savings arrangements established by States for non-governmental employees.

22. **Signed** on May 16, 2017

    H.R. 274 - Modernizing Government Travel Act

23. **Signed** on May 12, 2017

    S. 496 -An Act to repeal the rule issued by the Federal Highway Administration and the Federal Transit Administration entitled "Metropolitan Planning Organization Coordination and Planning Area Reform".

24. **Signed** on May 8, 2017

    H.R. 534 - U.S. Wants to Compete for a World Expo Act

25. **Signed** on May 5, 2017

    H.R. 244 - Consolidated Appropriations Act, 2017

26. **Signed** on April 28, 2017

    H.J. Res. 99 - Joint Resolution making further continuing appropriations for fiscal year 2017, and for other purposes.

27. **Signed** on April 19, 2017

    S.J.Res. 36 - Joint Resolution providing for the appointment of Roger W. Ferguson as a citizen regent of the Board of Regents of the Smithsonian Institution.

28. Signed on April 19, 2017

S.J.Res. 35 - Joint Resolution providing for the appointment of Michael Govan as a citizen regent of the Board of Regents of the Smithsonian Institution.

29. Signed on April 19, 2017

S.J.Res. 30 - Joint Resolution providing for the reappointment of Steve Case as a citizen regent of the Board of Regents of the Smithsonian Institution.

30. Signed on April 19, 2017

S. 544 - An Act to amend the Veterans Access, Choice, and Accountability Act of 2014 to modify the termination date for the Veterans Choice Program, and for other purposes.

31. Signed on April 18, 2017

H.R. 353 - Weather Research and Forecasting Innovation Act of 2017

32. Signed on April 13, 2017

H.J. Res. 67 - Joint Resolution disapproving the rule submitted by the Department of Labor relating to savings arrangements established by qualified State political subdivisions for non-governmental employees.

33. Signed on April 13, 2017

H.J. Res. 43 - Joint Resolution providing for congressional disapproval under chapter 8 of title 5, United States Code, of the final rule submitted by Secretary of Health and Human Services relating to compliance with title X requirements by project...

34. **Signed** on April 3, 2017

S.J.Res. 34 - Joint Resolution providing for congressional disapproval under chapter 8 of title 5, United States Code, of the rule submitted by the Federal Communications Commission relating to "Protecting the Privacy of Customers of Broadband...

35. **Signed** on April 3, 2017

H.R. 1228 - An Act to provide for the appointment of members of the Board of Directors of the Office of Compliance to replace members whose terms expire during 2017, and for other purposes.

36. **Signed** on April 3, 2017

H.J. Res. 83, which nullifies the Department of Labor's rule titled Clarification of Employer's Continuing Obligation to Make and Maintain an Accurate Record of Each Recordable Injury and Illness; and

37. **Signed** on April 3, 2017

H.J. Res. 69, which nullifies the Department of the Interior's Fish and Wildlife Service's final rule relating to non-subsistence takings of wildlife on National Wildlife Refuges in Alaska

38. **Signed** on March 31, 2017

S.J.Res.1 - Joint Resolution approving the location of a memorial to commemorate and honor the members of the Armed Forces who served on active duty in support of Operation Desert Storm or Operation Desert Shield.

39. Signed on March 31, 2017

H.R.1362 - An Act to name the Department of Veterans Affairs community-based outpatient clinic in Pago Pago, American Samoa, the Faleomavaega Eni Fa'aua'a Hunkin VA Clinic.

40. Signed on March 31, 2017

H.J.Res.42 - Joint Resolution disapproving the rule submitted by the Department of Labor relating to drug testing of unemployment compensation applicants.

41. Signed on March 28, 2017

S. 305 - Vietnam War Veterans Recognition Act of 2017

42. Signed on March 27, 2017

H.J.Res.57 - Providing for congressional disapproval under chapter 8 of title 5, United States Code, of the rule submitted by the Department of Education relating to accountability and State plans under the Elementary and Secondary Education Act of 1965.

43. Signed on March 27, 2017

H.J. Res. 58 - Joint Resolution providing for congressional disapproval under chapter 8 of title 5, United States Code, of the rule submitted by the Department of Education relating to teacher preparation issues.

43. Signed on March 27, 2017

H.J. Res. 44 - Joint Resolution disapproving the rule submitted by the Department of the Interior relating to Bureau of Land Management regulations that establish the procedures used to prepare, revise, or amend land use plans pursuant to the Federal Land

44. **Signed** on March 21, 2017

   S.442 - National Aeronautics and Space Administration Transition Authorization Act of 2017

45. **Signed** on March 13, 2017

   H.R.609 - To designate the Department of Veterans Affairs health care center in Center Township, Butler County, Pennsylvania, as the "Abie Abraham VA Clinic".

46. **Signed** on February 28, 2017

   H.R. 321 - Inspiring the Next Space Pioneers, Innovators, Researchers, and Explorers (INSPIRE) Women Act

47. **Signed** on February 28, 2017

   H.R. 255 - Promoting Women in Entrepreneurship Act

48. **Signed** on February 28, 2017

   H.J. Res. 40 - Joint Resolution providing for congressional disapproval under chapter 8 of title 5, United States Code, of the rule submitted by the Social Security Administration relating to Implementation of the NICS Improvement Amendments Act of 2007.

49. **Signed** on February 16, 2017

   H.J.Res.38 - Disapproving the rule submitted by the Department of the Interior known as the Stream Protection Rule.

50. **Signed** on February 14, 2017

H.J.Res.41 - Providing for congressional disapproval under chapter 8 of title 5, United States Code, of a rule submitted by the Securities and Exchange Commission relating to "Disclosure of Payments by Resource Extraction Issuers".

51. **Signed** on January 31, 2017

H.R.72 - GAO Access and Oversight Act of 2017

52. **Signed** on January 20, 2017

S.84 - A bill to provide for an exception to a limitation against appointment of persons as Secretary of Defense within seven years of relief from active duty as a regular commissioned officer of the Armed Forces.

President Trump Likes to Take Credit for Jobs

Here Are the Facts

One of many campaign promises Donald Trump made was to pass legislation that would promote more jobs for American citizens. He proudly proclaimed throughout news media outlets that his negotiation skills were an effective approach used as a tool to negotiate deals that would encourage companies to remain in America as opposed to relocating overseas. Although sources indicate that some American company reactions to his offer were encouraging, there are some pertinent facts that should be considered.

What You Need to Know – Fact Check

According to the Bureau of Labor Statistics there are over 50 thousand coal mining jobs in the United States. Since Trump has been in office an additional 800 jobs were added in the coal mining field. In other areas such as the logging sector there was a significant increase of 42,000 jobs that occurred during the Obama years prior to Trumps presidency. The unemployment rate was 4.1, as of October 2017.

According to Dow Jones the Stock Market, is having an excellent time, since the election of President Trump.

Trump's 37% approval rating is also lower than majority of president in the history of modern polling at the same point in their tenure.

What We Need to Know

Electoral College. (2017). Retrieved from http:// www.history.com/topics/electoral-college

Historical Facts: Electoral College

During the Constitution Convention in 1787, delegates from Virginia proposed a plan that paved the way to change the way the President is elected in the United States. In this way, an Electoral College would be created thereby, providing congress with full authority to elect the President. After several debates, delegates from many states agreed and a committee was formed to iron out the details. A difficult and critical sticking point at the Constitutional Convention was how to count a state's population. Particularly controversial was how to count slaves for the purposes of representation and taxation.

Since millions of Black People were enslaved a decision had to be made to determine how they would be counted in the census. Subsequently, the 3/5 (three fifths) Compromise was instituted which included delegates from northern and southern states. Slave states would benefit from including slaves in the total numbers which would be used to determine the number of seats that states would have in the United States House of Representatives.
THE DEBATE

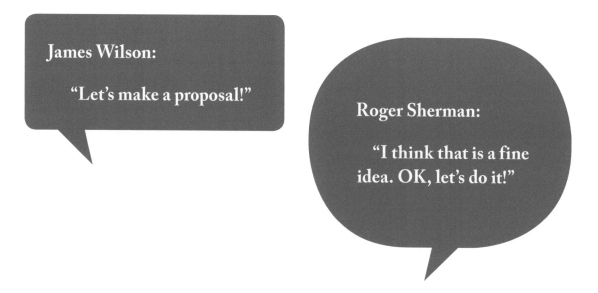

James Wilson:

"Let's make a proposal!"

Roger Sherman:

"I think that is a fine idea. OK, let's do it!"

Thomas Jefferson:

"The southern states will be taxed according to their population numbers and their wealth while the northern states will be taxed on the population numbers only!"

Supportive Delegate:

"White leaders in slave states would have more representatives in the House and the Electoral College. Therefore, we want slaves to be counted in our actual census numbers!"

Opposition Delegate

"Only free inhabitants of each state will be counted for appointment purposes!"

Large Population of Slave States Delegate:

"Slaves should be considered as persons when representation is determined but as property if the new government were to levy taxes on the basis of population!'

Small Population of Slave States Delegate:

"If the new government levies taxes then slaves should be included in taxation but not in determining representation!"

3/5 (three fifths) Compromise (Continued)- It is found in Article 1 section 2 page 3 of the United States Constitution. This is a portion of the article which reads as follows:

Article I, Section 2, also creates the way in which congressional districts are to be divided among the states.

Did you know that "if slaves were considered property, they would not be counted at all. If they were considered people, they would be counted fully — just as women, children and other non-voters were counted".

And, "southern slave-owners viewed slaves as property, but they wanted them to be fully counted in order to increase their political power in Congress".

Furthermore:

After extended debate, the framers agreed to the three-fifths compromise — each slave would equal three-fifths of a person in a state's population count. (Note: The framers did not use the word slave in the document.) After the Civil War, the formula was changed with the passage of the 13th Amendment, which abolished slavery, and Section 2 of the 14th Amendment, which repealed the three-fifths rule. This section also establishes that every 10 years, every adult in the country must answer a survey - a monumental task when people move as often as they do and when some people have no homes at all. Based on the surveys, Congress must determine how many representatives (at least one required) are to come from each state and how federal resources are to be distributed among the states. The Constitution set the number of House members from each of the original 13 states that were used until the first census was completed.

Did you know that: George Washington was elected Constitution Convention President in 1787?

What Do We Know?

The final decision was made to refer to slaves as "All Other Persons". They were considered as 3/5 (three fifths of the state actual numbers thereby reducing the representation of slave states). One of the ways to get slaves states to buy in or to go along with this compromise was to connect it with a taxation ratio so states received a reduction in taxes. Consequently, slave states had a disproportionate representation before the Civil War (1793) which influenced office of the President, Speaker of the House of Representatives and Supreme Court Nominations.

Should the Electoral College be abolished? What are people saying about this?

"I want to introduce a bill to get rid of the Electoral College!" Senator Barbara Boxer (7/31/17, Washington Examiner)

"We want to get rid of it too!" Democrats in the Senate and House of Representatives

Bill Nelson, Bernie Sanders, Dick Durbin, Steve Cohen, Julia Branley and many more

19% of Republicans in the House and Senate do not want to get rid of the Electoral College. (www.gallup.com)

What We Need to Know

After the Civil War

Section 2 of the 14th Amendment (1868) superseded article 1 section 2 clause 3 and repealed the Connecticut Compromise it read; "Representatives shall be apportioned… counting the whole number of persons in each state, excluding Indians not taxed. The 13th amendment of 1865 banned slavery but prisoners serving lifetime sentences were subject to the original section 2 of the 14th Amendment.

Who Are the Electors?

Let's Examine this more closely

Fact 1 – Electors are controlled by political parties in each state. Parties nominate potential electors at state party conventions or chose them by a vote of the party's central committee.

Fact 2 – One Exception

Nebraska and Maine have proportional distribution of electors. The state winner receives 2 electors and the winner of each congressional district receives 1 elector.

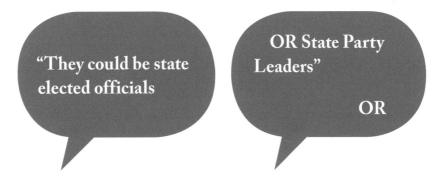

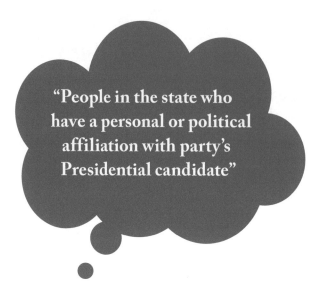

Fact 3 - There are no Restrictions on who electors can vote for.

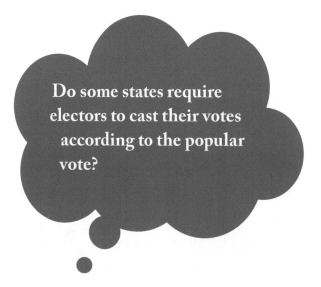

These pledges fall into 2 categories. Electors bound by state law and those bound by pledges to political parties.

Some state laws provide so called, "Faithless Electors" who could have to pay fines and may be disqualified. There are no supreme court rulings for not voting at all.

Retrieved from www.gallup.com/poll

III- States which predominately vote Democratic/Blue States

2016 Gallup Poll: Top 10

Hawaii – 24%

District of Columbia -64%

Maryland -23%

Rhode Island – 23%

New York-22%

Massachusetts -20%

Connecticut -17%

Vermont -17%

Illinois – 17%, Delaware-16%

"In the United States Blue states outnumber Red states 20-12".

"Do some states require electors to cast their votes according to the popular vote?"

"These pledges fall into 2 categories, Electors bond by state law and those bound by pledges to political parties. Some state laws provide so called, "Faithless Electors" who have to pay fines and may be disqualified. There are no Supreme Court rulings for not voting at all" (Gallup Poll, 2016)

What We Need to Know?

According to the United States census, each state is allocated a number of electors equal to the number of its senators which is always two plus the number of House of Representatives which may change according to the size of each state's population as determined in the census.

For example:

2016 Election Results As Per 2010 United States Census	
OHIO	18
OKLAHOMA	7
OREGON	7
PENNSYLVANIA	20
ALABAMA	9
NORTH CAROLINA	15
NEW YORK	29
CALIFORNIA	35

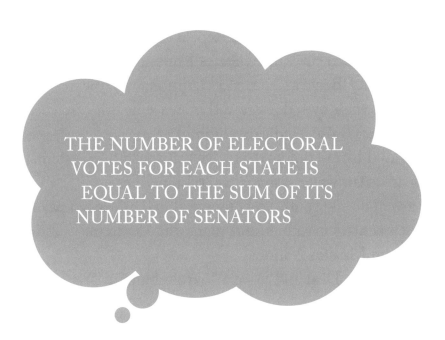

THE NUMBER OF ELECTORAL VOTES FOR EACH STATE IS EQUAL TO THE SUM OF ITS NUMBER OF SENATORS

Retrieved from www. http://state.keydata.com

President Elect Donald Trump Campaign Promises

- Expand the Economy by 6% (It was later decreased to 3%)
- Close Donald Trump Foundation to Eliminate Conflicts of Interest (New York State Attorney says it is under investigation and cannot be dissolved)
- Anti-Abortion Bill –Protect and Defend Conception
- (Donald Trump wants to get rid of pro-choice)
- Mitch McConnell (Speaker of the House) wants to get rid of the "Protecting Women's Rights Bill" put forth my former President Barack Obama
- Rowe verses Wade – At Risk for Being Overturned
- Repair tortured United States relations with Russia
- Repeal and Replace the Affordable care Act

- Pull out of the Paris Climate deal and Repeal former President Barack Obama ERA regulations designed to cut United States Emissions
- Cut Social Security Benefits and end traditional Medicare making it harder for seniors to choose their own doctors and increase health care costs for both current and future retirees; Raise Medicare eligibility age
- Proposes to Build Infrastructure to revive transportation systems, bridges, tunnels, electricity grid, clean water systems and oil pipelines
- Construct a wall on the southern border and make Mexico pay for it
- Expel undocumented migrants and plans for "Extreme" vetting of visitors and immigrants from Muslim Nations
- Renegotiate the Iran Deal and drive a "harder bargain"

Fact – Rowe vs Wade – Roe sued the Texas court by challenging the constitutionality of the abortion laws in December 13, 1971. The case was based on allegations that contraceptive failure could result in "unpreparedness for parenthood and impairment of the women's health". It was argued on December, 1971 and decided by the courts on January 22, 1993.

Rowe vs. Wade. (1973). Retrieved from http://caselaw.find/law.com/us-supreme-court/410/113.html

What Does this Mean and How Could this affect You and Your family?

- ❖ Rich Get Richer
- ❖ Privatizing Medicare and Social Security; Dismantle Medicaid
- ❖ An "all out" war on women's health care and reproductive freedom
- ❖ Echoing history's darkest chapters by denying Muslim refugees entry to America based on their religious beliefs
- ❖ Repeal of Obamacare would lead to 20 million people losing health insurance, premiums increasing significantly, seniors not being able to afford prescriptions

❖ Climate Change Deniers could result in dismantling environmental protections and endangering our planet.

Let's Break this down even more!

The House Minority leader, Nancy Pelosi reported that 24 million American lives could be in jeopardy that depends on a Social Security check to supplement income. Moreover, some seniors, the Social Security check are their only source of income. In addition, those who rely on Medicare could also be affected. Trump plans to privatize Medicare and Social Security and Medicaid which was one of his campaign promises.

Trump intends to sign a bill to defund Planned Parenthood. This program provides services to 2.5 million women such as: reproductive health care, education and outreach. According to a Planned Parenthood article, one out of five women utilizes Parent Parenthood services for Pap Tests, breast exams, and preventative sexually transmitted disease testing. Planned Parenthood. (2017). Retrieved from: https:// www.plannedparenthood.org

If the Republicans succeed in replacing and repealing the Affordable Care Act and replace it with the so called, "Trumpcare" 24 million Americans could lose their health coverage.

Update: <u>Trumps proposed budget cuts could also negatively affect families including</u>:

- Slash 4.7 billion in the Department of Agriculture
- Cut federal Support For Rural Airports
- Cut Meals on Wheels and Millions of Seniors Relay on this Program
- Cut After-School Programs including Aids to Boost Academic Growth and Achievement; 1.6 million students benefit from Afterschool Programs
- Affordable Housing for Seniors
- Cut $4,000,000,000,000 (Four Billion Dollars) in Pell Grants and college prep programs that help students remain in college
- Cut programs to National Health Institutes curtailing needed research
- Cut SEOG (A federal Supplemental Educational Opportunity Grant) which helps many students pay for college

Note: 30 million dollars is spent per month to maintain Trump Tower 3.1 Seniors of which 500, 000 are veterans and 3.6% of all homeless people are veterans

Six million people could lose the benefits of the Low Income Housing Home Energy Assistant Program (LIHEAP) that provide supplemental monetary support in order to help ease the financial burden of energy bills.

Reports indicate that approximately 50 programs and loss of jobs could be impacted after Trump cuts funding for the Environmental Protection Agency (EPA) that protects and maintain clean air and water.

Multi-millionaires – Draining the Swamp? Oligarchs?

Donald Trump Cabinet Picks

Trump's idea of a so-called "Draining the Swamp" is to rid the country of Washington establishment. He believes this means lobbyists, campaign, donors, and any corruption. Unfortunately, he has not been successful. In fact, his cabinet picks are relatively swampy. Let's examine this more closely.

What We Need to Know

Note: Although Trump is imposing lobbying bans, his cabinet picks are full of lobbyists. Below are the list Trump's cabinet appointees who gave 6 million or more to Trump and his Super PACS in the 2016 election cycle.

Trumps Cabinet Appointments (2017). Retrieved from www.mcclatchydc.com/news/politics-government)

1. **Rex Tillerson** – Secretary of State- Formerly head of Exxon Mobil and the American Petroleum Institute member of the Business Roundtable. He has spent $364.4 million on lobbying and contributing to Trumps campaign and Republican candidates such as Speaker Paul Ryan, Jeb Bush, George W, Bush, and Senate Majority Leader Mitch McConnell.

Note: Tillerson is the first secretary of state with no government or military experience. It is alleged that he has strong business ties with Vladimer Putin.

2. **Linda McMahon** – Administrator of the Small Business Administration. McMahon has contributed $20,000,000 or more for Republican candidates and more than 6 million to Trump's campaign. (Source: www.abcnews.com)

3. **Betsy Devos** – Secretary of Education – Devos contributed 7.8 million or more to Republican candidates and 1.8 million to the Republican Party and Trump's campaign.

4. **Andy Putzer** – Secretary of Labor – According to Sources, Putzer and his wife contributed more than $330 thousand to Trump's campaign and the Republican National Committee.

5. **Carl Icahn** – Special Advisor on Regulatory Reform – Contributed $6,000,000 or more.

6. **Steve Munuchin** – Treasury Secretary – Munuchin was Trump's campaign chairman who helped raise money for Trump thereby increasing the number of donors.

Note: Munuchin is a Wall Street investor billionaire (former One West Bank CEO) and hedge Fund Manager. Sources indicate he is a close friend of Donald Trump.

7. **Tom Price** – Secretary of Health and Human Services – Contributed $6,000.000 or more.

8. **Mike Pompeo** – Director of the Central Intelligence Agency – Contributed $6,000.000 or more to Trump's campaign.

9. **Wilbur Ross** – Secretary of Commerce – Billionaire Investor in Steel, Coal Mining, and Textile industries - Ross supported Trump during the campaign

by contributing $6,000.000 or more to the Republican National Committee and according to reports he also helped Trump avoid bankruptcy.

What We Need To Know

Trump's Travel Ban Ruling – February 9, 2017

A Hawaiian court prevented Trump's travel ban to continue. Sources say that he will most likely have to go to the U. S. Supreme Court since there are two federal appeal courts involved. The first one was in San Francisco and the other in Richmond Virginia. In an effort to win his appeals, he revised the travel ban by removing the preference for refugees who are religious minorities and gave exemptions to green card holders and those who already hold Visas. Iraq was also removed from the list.

News media networks and print Media in Support of Trump (2017). Retrieved from http://nymag.com

Rupert Murdoch
Rupert Murdoch, the former CEO of Fox Network supported Trump's campaign. This was in sharp contrast to his earlier nod to Megyn Kelly (a popular journalist on Fox news network who most recently moved to NBC News) to "hammer" Trump during the GOP debate. Immediately after the debate Trump insulted her in a tweet rant. According to New York Magazine.com both Kelly and Trump had a truce during a private meeting prompted by Trump's son-in-law, Jared Kushner.

Trump's Campaign Manager, Kelly Ann Conway

http://www.cosmopolitan.com/politics- Michael Sebastian, 3/20/17

Kellyanne Conway became the first woman campaign manager for a republican candidate. She's married with four children. She spent most of her political career as a surrogate and advisor for the Republican Party. She focused primarily on how to attract female voters. Conway was a long- time friend of Trump since 2006. She initially worked on Senator Ted Cruz (a 2017 presidential candidate) campaign. As counselor to the President, she is currently the highest-ranking woman in the White House. Sources indicate Conway coined terms like, "fake news" and "alternative facts" to obscure the truth. In fact, she has been banned from appearing on one of the MSNBC shows called, "Morning Joe" because of her alleged misinterpretation of the facts. She worked for Newt Gingrich who is an ardent supporter of Trump. Conway spent most of her life in politics. In the 1970's she received a law degree in Political Science and for many years supported the Republican Party. Michael S. (2017). Trump's Campaign Manager, Kelly Ann Conway.

Retrieved from http://www.cosmopolitan.com/politics

<u>What is Racism?</u> Extrinsic Racism Remarks made by Trump: Sexism, Homophobia, and the LGBT Community
Cohen, Claire. (2017). Donald Trump Sexism Tracker: Every Offensive Comment in one Place. Retrieved from The Telegraph Lifestyle/Women

Sexism is defined as: discriminatory or abusive behavior towards members of the opposite sex. Sexism [Def 1]. (n.d.). vocabulary.com dictionary. Retrieved from https://www.vocabularycom/dictionary/sexism

Donald Trump has used insidious remarks to describe women especially women who either refused his passes or speak out against him. Words like the following: I have a "fat picture" of her in my desk drawer.

1991: Trump called women "beautiful pieces of ass".
1992: He was quoted saying, "You have to treat women like shit"
1993: "You have to grab them by the Pussy"
1994: "When I come home and dinner's not ready, I go through the roof!"
1997: "I get bored when women become successful, they are like gold-diggers"
1997: "I could have nailed Princess Di"
1999: "I have a deal with her (referencing his daughter, Ivanka Trump). She's 17 and doing great! She made me promise to never date a girl younger than her. So as she grows older, the field is getting very limited"
2003: Referencing his daughter Ivanka-"She's got the best body and I helped create her"
2006: If Ivanka weren't my daughter, perhaps I'd be dating her"

__What You Need to Know__: 45% of College Educated White Women Voted for Donald Trump

Breakdown: 20% white women college grads; 17% white women with no degree; 17% white men college grads; 17% white men with no degree: 29% non-whites. CNN Exit Polls. (2016). retrieved from: http/www.cnn.com

__Terms You Need to Know__

__Racism__: an empowering relationship between two groups where one group can use their power, wealth, and resources to control another group. In 1638, the state of Maryland put an edict public policy exclusion) which later became the doctrine of racism called, The Doctrine of Exclusion 1638-1665.

Source: Dr. Claude Andersen

Extrinsic Racism: There is a moral component to the essence of a race which warrants differentiated treatment. These differences are to the extrinsic racist, not particularly controversial. http://www.mdcbowen.org

Intrinsic Racism: Race and Racism – 11/3/14 – Extrinsic and Intrinsic Racism and Cultural Racisms. Anthony Appiah, 1990 "Racisms": University of Minnesota Press. "The moral essence of a race establishes an incontrovertible status for the race no matter what an individual member of a race no matter what an individual member of a race does he should be treated just like the rest of his race.

Incontrovertible meaning- (not able to be denied or disputed; synonym: undeniable; irrefutable; incontestable)

Donald Trumps demonstrated racialism by stating" Black people have nothing to lose; they all live in crime-ridden neighborhoods, and can get shot just walking down the street". Trump blames crime on Black people. Huffington Post. http://www.huffintongpost.com.

Is this an example of Extrinsic or Intrinsic Racism? Trump excluded Black people from all other races in his commentary. He specifically targeted Black people only which implies that crime problems are exclusive to Black pole and ono other race.

"No matter what an individual member of a race does he /she should be treated like the rest of the race" One size fits all!"
Huffington Post. (June, 5, 2013). Latino Voices. Retrieved from http:/www.huffington post.com

Trump tweeted the majority of crimes are committed by Blacks and Hispanics. He was quoted saying Mexicans are Murderers and rapists and this s also was his reasoning behind building a border wall and force the Mexican government to pay for it during his campaign.

However, now the story is different since he has been in office and the American taxpayers will have to pay for it.

Update: Trump threatens a government shutdown if Congress does not provide funding to pay for the wall. Hulse, C. (2017).Trump Fences himself in with border wall spending threat". Retrieved from https://www.nytimes.com/2017/08/24/us/politics/trump-wall-government-shutdown-congress.html

Is this an example of racism, or sexism? Trump: "If Hillary Clinton can't satisfy her husband then what makes her think she can satisfy America?

Note: Every one of Donald Trump's cabinet picks opposes equal rights for gays and lesbians. Many Supreme Court picks also oppose LGBT (Lesbians, Gays, Bi-Sexual, and Transgender) rights. Wenninger, E. (9/9/15). Homophobic- Donald Trump promote a racist, sexist, and homophobic agenda. Retrieved from http://www.idsnews.com.

Immigration Policy

What We Need to Know – History

One hundred years ago the 1917 Immigration Act categorized any person form the Asian and Pacific zone as "Undesirables". The sub-categories included "epileptics" (mentally and physically defective). The ban excluded any persons from the *"Asiatic barred Zone"*. Retrieved from www. http://daily.jstor.org/1917 The only Europeans allowed to the United States were people who were not "undesirable" and had to pass a literacy test. The Asians were prevented from coming to the United States due to a so-called threat to job security.

Canada also had an exclusionary policy in 1908 called, Continuous Journey Law: This allowed people to enter the United States only if they were coming directly from their native land. South Asian people were banned. Canada did not provide a direct path to its country so it kept out immigrants from India. But many Indians migrated to Seattle and San Francisco. _Was this overt discrimination? Why? Why Not?_

Statistical Data on Crimes Committed in the United States by Mexicans

What We Need to Know–History

Mexico became a part of the United States after 1854. Mexicans were forced off their lands through treaties, war, and land purchases. In 1890, 75,000 Mexicans came to the United States as cheap laborers. After the Great depression of 1920, 80,000 Mexicans came to the United States and some of them without their families. Retrieved from factcheck.org/

Note: 80% of the United States population is immigrants

1.6% of the state and federal prison population is under Immigration and Customs Enforcement (I.C.E.) jurisdiction. One half of prisoners are in custody for various crimes and 10.7% of prisoners in federal jails were incarcerated for immigration defenses in 2009. 2% are sex offenders. Pew: In 2005, 11.1 million illegal immigrants live in the United States. I.C.E. (Department of Justice [DOJ], n.d.). Retrieved from https://www. Justice.gov/

How Many Groups Immigrated to America?

Fact Check: Research indicated that immigrants entering the united Sates since the early 1900's **_has not had any_** significant impact on increasing or decreasing the crime rate. Immigration and Crime. (n.d.). In Wikipedia. Retrieved from Wikipedia. https://en.wikipedia.org/wiki/Immigration_and_crime

History: In the 17th century, 400,000 English people migrated to Colonial America as indentured servants. In 1836-1914, there were over 30 million Europeans migrated to the United States. During the middle of the 19th century, 1,285,349 immigrants came from northern Europe. These countries include: Denmark, Estonia, Finland, Iceland, Ireland, Latvia, Lithuania, Sweden, and the United Kingdom. During the early 20th century, immigrants came from southern and eastern Europe including, southern France, Italy, Sicily, Albania, Portugal, eastern Russia, Ukraine, Turkey, Romania, Bulgaria, Cyprus (Mediterranean Countries) and Malta. Before 1965, mostly Latin American and Asian immigrants migrated to the United States.

Note: The Chinese Exclusion Act of 1882 banned almost all immigration from China until it was repealed in 1943.

In 1921 the United States Congress passed the Emergency Quota Act in order to prevent immigrants from southern and eastern Europe such as Jews, Italians, and Slavs (one of a group of peoples in eastern, southern Slavs and Central Europe including the Russians, Ruthenians, Bulgars, Serbs, Croats, Slavonians, Poles, Czechs, Moravians, and Slovaks)

1929-There were 279,678 immigrants in the U.S.
1933-There were 23,068 immigrants in the U.S.
1930-The United States saw a decrease in the number of people migrating to the United States.

What We Need to Know

The United States had a repatriation program to deport Mexicans who wanted to stay in the United States. It was called Mexican Repatriation. The purpose was to encourage them to return to their homelands by many did not want to go. 400,000 Mexicans were deported. Also the United States restricted many Jewish refugees who escaped the Nazis during World War II but the United States banned them from entering the country. After the war, the United States had yet another initiative to deport Mexicans in 1954. 1,075,168 were forced to return to their homelands involuntarily. During this time, Ted Kennedy was Chief Senate sponsor of the Immigration and Nationality Act of 1965.

Note: In 1986- President Ronald Reagan gave amnesty to 3 million undocumented immigrants

In 2012 and 2014, President Barack Obama put in place policies that would minimize deportation by using "Anchor Babies" as a "means of migrating to the United States" (U.S. Census Bureau 2017)

Anchor Babies- American born children of Immigrants

2000-14 million immigrants entered the United States
2013-Immigrants mostly came from China, Mexico, and India
2011-Over I million legal residents

Note: Donald Trump suspends entry to the United States from several countries including Syria, Iran, Somalia, Sudan, Yemen, and Libya. This was a revised travel ban of which Iraq was removed from the list. Source: USA today. 3/6/17 Title: Trump issues revised ban for 6 majority Muslim countries

Donald Trumps' Relationship with (KKK) Klu Klux Klan and Alternative Right Extremist Groups

During the campaign, there were several reports about Donald Trumps' support from White Neo-Nazis and other groups associated with the Klu Klux Klan. Many of these groups vocally express their resentment against Jews and people of color including Blacks. Racists such as the notorious Klan leader, David Duke, and Andrew Anglin, who is the publisher of the Neo-Nazi site called the "Daily Stormer". These men rallied around Donald Trumps' candidacy. Donald Trump has been consistent with the Anti-immigrant rhetoric which has been the magnet attracting their interests. A flurry of Donald Trumps' surrogates and mouth pieces hit the air waves to denounce the White nationalist support for him such as his campaign spokesman, Jason Miller but there were many others who rebuked these comments to the contrary (Berger, 2016).

In fact, according to (Berger, 2016) "there was an unprecedented unified support for a modern major party nominee". Some of these hate groups saturate the internet highways such as the Reddit Network defined as a "huge online bulletin board" (Berger, 2016). It is associated with a media mogul called Conde' Nast, owners of Vanity Fair, The New Yorker and many other online publications with more than 90 million consumers. Its largest shareholder is Advance Publications. Chimpire, GreatApes, and Coontown are just a few of the anti-Black propaganda that is a driving force for White supremacists in this country. Donald Trumps' candidacy and now his presidency has given rise to these hate mongers that is unprecedented. Moreover, 64% of White males voted for Trump and according to Berger, 2016, a large percentage were White hate groups who believe "Donald Trump represents our interests" which is the first time many of them voted in any election. (Berger, 2016)

Breakdown of Americans Who Voted For Donald Trump

(further explored)

<u>*Amongst the White Evangelical Voters the major reasons were*</u>:

a) Love of the Tea Party (a conservative movement within the Republican Party) Ideology
b) Smaller Government
c) Creating Jobs
d) Deporting Illegal Immigrants

One reporter argued there are many people who call themselves Evangelical but never go to church and only use the Evangelical title as a religious decoy. 81% of Evangelicals voted for Trump. Why Many Conservatives Have Lined up Behind Trump. (2017). Retrieved from http://www.urbanchristiannews.com

Tyson, A., & Maniam, S. (2016, November 9). Behind Trumps' Victory: Divisions by Race, Gender and Education. Pew Research Center Retrieved from http:// www.perresearch.org

White Non- Hispanic Voters- 21%; Democrats 37%; Republican 58%
White Men – 53% ; Democrats – 44%
Without a College degree – 52%; Democrats 44%
Whites without a College Degree – 67%; Democrats -28%
Whites with a College Degree – 49%; Democrats 45%
Young Voters – 55%; Democrats -37%
Older Voters 65 and Older – 53%; Democrats 45%

How Many Democrats crossed over and Voted for Donald Trump?

Olsen, H. (2016, November 21). Can the Republican Party Keep Trump Dems? National Review. Retrieved from http://www.nationalreview.com

White Non-College educated Democrats and Independents- Michigan 12,000; Wisconsin- 10 White historically Democratic counties; Iowa –every eastern county that was mostly Democrat.

Trump and Putin Relationship (*What else you need to know*)

Marine Le Pen was a Presidential candidate in France Italy. She was described as a "far right" candidate who had similar views as Donald Trump and Vladimir Putin, Russian President. During her campaign, Le pen vowed to ban immigrants from France, specifically Muslims. She had White Supremacists support namely from Klansmen David Duke who endorsed Donald Trump. Throughout Trumps' campaign and during his first 100 days as President, he publically supported Vladimir Putin by defending him against allegations of killing journalist in his country. In addition, one of Trumps' campaign promises was to pull out of NATO (North Atlantic Treaty Organization between several North American and European states based on a North Atlantic Treaty that was signed on April 4, 1949) which is also what Le Pen promised to do during her campaign and this is quite similar to Putin's views. Finally, Putin would like Trump to eliminate sanctions that were imposed on Russia under the Obama administration however, Trump did not comply.

Updates: Donald Trump signed the sanctions bill against Russia on in August 2017 but he was quoted saying, "the bill remains seriously flawed". Collins, Herb, Diaz, 2017). Trump signs bill approving new sanctions against Russia. (2017, August 3). Retrieved from cnn.com

Marine Le Pen lost the French presidential election to Emmanuel Macron.

Steve Bannon and Trump (architect of the anti-globalist policies)

"Let's dig a little deeper

Kevin, D. (2016). Is Steve Bannon Racist? Let's Find Out! Retrieved from www. motherjones.com

Eric, H. (2017). Media Matters- Breibart Reporter- Is a White Nationalist with a Long Trail of Racist and Anti-Muslim Twitter.

Breibart News Defined: a famed right wing news site that traffics racism, anti-Semitism, and anti-immigration hysteria.

Steve Bannon is notorious for his Breibart News which is a White racist Nationalist radio station. He attached himself to Donald Trump because he believed he too represents White Nationalist views. Breibart reporters have a long history of promoting racist and anti-Muslimism rhetoric. In fact, according to one source, Black and Arab people are inherently more violent than any other groups which are attributed to their low IQ's (Intelligence Quotient). Hispanics are equally as violent not because of low IQ (Intelligence Quotient) but because they are "descendants of Aztecs and Incas". With all the rhetoric about the "Alt Right" (Alternative Right) the Southern Poverty Law Center (SPLC) reported that Steve Bannon, formerly CEO of Breibart news and now Chief Strategist and Senior Counselor is the center of this racist ideology. The (SPLC) defined the "Alt Right" as:

A set of far-right ideologies, groups and individuals whose core belief is that "white identity" is under attack by multicultural forces using "political correctness" and "social justice" to undermine white people and "their" civilization. Characterized by heavy use of social media and online memes, Alt-Righters eschew "establishment" conservatism, skew young, and embrace white ethno-nationalism as a fundamental value. Retrieved from https://www.splcenter.org/fighting-hate/extremist-files/ideology/alternative-right (n.d)

According to the "Mother Jones" article, the mere fact that Donald Trump picked Steve Bannon to assume a post in his Administration speaks volumes about his willingness to support a man who has a proven track record of hate towards certain groups of people in this country and around the worked is unconscionable. This action has also sent a signal to White Supremacist groups like the KKK (Klu Klux Klan) who has glorified Trump as their savior and champion". (Drum 2016). Steve Bannon's Breibart news, KKK and neo Nazi White Supremacist groups are growing in numbers largely due to White young males who are vehemently opposed to immigration, multiculturalism, feminism and political correctness. This implies that although they express hate mongering propaganda using social media, television and other outlets, it is ok and an "art of freedom" (Nguyen 2017)

This is in line with Donald Trumps' hateful rhetoric against Black, Mexicans, Muslims, and immigrants since he began his campaign in 2016. The synergy between Steve Bannon and Donald Trump is a dangerous mixture of non-political correctness of White Nationalism propaganda. A government transformation this country does not need!

Update: Trump removed Steve Bannon as his Chief Strategist. Tina N. (2017). Steve Bannon is leaving the White House. Retrieved from www.vanityfair.com/news

Trump's Tax Proposal – Goal: To get to 3% growth overall which according to reports is a fantasy.

Mark, E. (2017). What it means for the rich, the world and for you. Retrieved from

Cut Corporate Rate to 15%

Eliminate Alternative Minimum Tax

Repeal Estate Tax

What Does This Mean?

Reduce deductions for Child Care

Bigger tax cut for the ultra- wealthy

Eliminate all deductions except mortgage and charitable giving

Reduce seven tax brackets to three

Repeal ACA (Affordable Care Act) 3.8% tax on investment income

Tax plan cuts corporate rates

Taxation on imports

Trump and Sanctuary Cities

Somin reports that Sanctuary Cities (cities should assist the federal government in enforcing immigration law) that do not comply with the federal government mandates according to section 1733 which states:

Federal, state, or local government entity or official may not prohibit, or in any way restrict, any governmental entity or official from sending to, or receiving from the immigration and naturalization service information regarding the citizenship or immigration status, lawful or unlawful, of any individual- (Federal Statue 1373). Iva S. (2017). Trump's order on Sanctuary Cities is Dangerous and an Unconstitutional Source. Retrieved from www.learnliberty.org

What We Need to Know

Some argue that Sanctuary Cities shield or protect illegal immigrants. While others argue the federal government is stepping out of bounds by forcing state and local governments to do their dirty work. It brings into question whether it is constitutional to restrict grant funding from states that do not comply with the law. Many cities refuse to detain immigrants in jails because of their status. Reports show that there are 168 counties in the United States where the majority of illegal immigrants reside. Sixty-nine of the counties complies with the law. (Immigration and Customs Enforcement Compliance Report, 2017)

What Does This Mean to You?

The Sanctuary Cities law can have serious consequences and implications   such as:

- It promotes racial profiling meaning local police are empowered to stop people at will based on skin color. This affects African Americans, Hispanics, and other people of color.
- It has implications of enforcing the Stop and Frisk policy (Here's how it works: See Below)

City Police pulls someone over and arrests him or her for something unrelated to citizenship such as, tail light out, drunken driving, expired sticker

The person is then booked into the local county jail which is usually run by the county sheriff's department. Joe Arpaio was formerly the Sheriff in Maricopa Arizona. He was found guilty on July 31, 2017 of criminal contempt by an Arizona judge. He took a hard line in enforcing

random traffic stops to screen illegal immigrants by conducting "patrol sweeps' which were done mainly in Hispanic areas. Source: The Republic. Azcentral.com Title: Former Maricopa County Sheriff Joe Arpaio guilty of criminal contempt (8/1/17)

Update: Sheriff Arpaio was pardoned by Donald Trump on 8/24/17

Fingerprints are taken and sent to the Federal Bureau of Investigations (FBI) and then to the United States Immigration and Customs Enforcement Department referred to as I.C.E.

If the person is undocumented then I.C.E. sends a request for the county jail to hold them for 48 hours in order to get a warrant.

The Department of Homeland Security reported counties do not have to detain individuals without a warrant because it is **unconstitutional** according to the 4th amendment of the United States Constitution. So their cooperation is **voluntary.**

Donald Trump's Relentless Cry to Lock Up Hillary Clinton

Although Trump won the electoral vote, Hillary Clinton won the popular vote he still incited the offensive chant from his supporters during many of his campaign rallies yelling, "Lock Her Up!" In fact, during one of his rallies (after the election) in Nashville, Tennessee according to NBC.News.com, he referenced Hillary once again when speaking to the crowd about his anger with a federal judge who blocked his immigrant travel ban and made verbal attacks against Hillary Clinton, the crowd chanted, "Lock her Up! Lock her Up!" He quoted, "Fortunately the former secretary of state is not in the White House!"

Many of his supporters sported T-Shirts with prison jail striped with slogans such as "Hillary for Prison". In a town in Iowa there was a "Hillary For Prison large float decorated with an orange jump suit depicting a prison uniform. Finally, reports indicated that Trump told Hillary during the presidential campaign that if he becomes President, he will appoint a special prosecutor and "you would be in jail" (Mother Jones, 2016)

Donald Trump and the Politics of Fear

Trump, according to reports is a master of fear mongering. He played on people anxieties and apprehensions about terrorism and crime. There are millions of people in the United States who believe they are victims and if not protected, they will easily become the victims. Donald trump capitalized on these fears during his campaign touting the possibility of terrorist attacks not only abroad but domestically which in his words are perpetrated from undocumented Mexican murderers and rapist. He also included Black people who are responsible for the violence and crimes in many of the urban districts across the country. Trump stated, "countless innocent American lives have been stolen because our politicians have failed in their duty to secure our borders".
Molly, (2016). Atlantic Magazine. Retrieved from www.theatlantic.com

One reporter, Reed Galon described his campaign rhetoric as "a fear-fueled acid trip". The real fear is the people who believe him. Instead of invoking fear, Donald Trump should inform American citizens that leaders around the world should develop and fully implement a strategic plan of cooperation for the benefit of everyone involved. Molly, B. (2016).

Studies show that violence has declined over the years. In a July 206 New York Times article, titled, "Donald Trump's Campaign Fear" one reporter wrote: "Trump is a poisonous messenger that an ossified party who dedicated itself to improving working people's lives, instead of serving the elite".

What We Need to Know

A number of reports show that although in 2014 violent crime increased, in 2015 violent crime totals were 0.7% lower in 20111 and 16.5% below the 2016 level. (www.fbi.gov 9/2016). The Huffington post published an article written by Christopher Mathaic on 1/28/17 wrote, "There have been zero fatal terror attacks on the United States since 1975 by immigrants" from the seven countries in Donald Trumps' travel ban that was announced to the American public before he removed Iraq. These six countries include Iran, Libya, Somalia, Sudan, Syria, and Yemen. Mathaic also noted that that 9/11 attackers were not from any of the countries listed that .Donald Trump banned from traveling to America. Lastly, the report indicated that Muslim Americans represent a tiny fraction of overall violence in the United States and Donald Trumps' fear mongering is exaggerated rhetoric at best.

Highlights from Donald Trump's First 30 Days in Office

Russia Investigation Draws Comparisons to Watergate

Impeachable Office- holding the President of the United States accountable for not only his acts but subordinates under his egis if there was an assault on the Constitution.

What We Need to Know

An impeachable offense is political as opposed to criminal

Abuse of Power – Article 2 of the U.S. Constitution reads that although evidence is not directly tied to the President, his subordinates can be under continuous investigation and he can be held accountable for allowing things to go on under his watch.

Donald Trump was sued by a group called, Citizens for Responsibility and Ethics in Washington D.C. regarding his business dealings.

DACA – Deferred Action for Childhood Arrivals. According to https://en.wikipedia. org/wiki/Deferred_Action_for_Childhood_Arrivals, 800,000 children enrolled in the program established by President Barack Obama in June 2011 but has been rescinded by the Trump Administration in September 2017.

Politics and Sexual Harassment

"We thought we were the Beacon of Morality"

In the United States, the abuse of females is nothing new. Female slaves, domestic servant, had to endure sexual harassment from their male bosses. Men who participate in raping women justified the unhealthy action on the females. Women carried the burden of being molested because of the clothes they wore and, for being permissive and unintelligent. As more and more women enter into the workplace, regardless of their skills level and the job they did, their ability to do the same job as their counterpart, they were considered the object of immature and insensitive bosses and co-workers. No matter how intelligent or educated women were, some men used their so-called male superiority and proudness, to justified unacceptable comments or inappropriate behaviors toward their female counterpart. As more and more women for economic, educational and self-fulfillment were successfully able to compete for challenging and rewarding employment. When females workers, starting demanding respect for the jobs they were doing, immature men's began to long for the days when they were in control of women physically and economically.

As Professional educators who have been in the workforce for many years, we are conscious of the impact inappropriate sexual behaviors have on both males and females' physics and their ability to perform in an environment where there is subtle justification for sexism, racism, and homophobia. From the employers' perspective, sexual harassment and other unacceptable behaviors is an unnecessary expense that affects institution's financial bottom line. However, some companies and organization do invest in employment-practices liability insurance (EPI). Why because inappropriate behaviors are projected to cost business and government entity appropriately $7 billion a year. However, some employers rely on traditional policies to provide coverage,

Did you know our government has ways of protecting itself from inappropriate disputes on Capitol Hill? Since 1997, appropriately 17 million dollars was paid to settle workplace disputes. Guess who foots the bill?

<u>*American Taxpayers!!*</u>

Conclusion

"The Election That Left Many Americans and Citizens from Around the World Confused"

This extraordinary book "What did you Know" before and after 2016 election was written to encourage individuals and groups to think about what they knew and did not know during the 2016 election and beyond. This book generates discussions about the 2016 election and aftermath in an educational format. This book is fascinating as well as useful in facilitating one's knowledge of political theory, politicians, methodology, and tactics utilized to gain people support, using the art of persuasion (Politics).

This book examines the struggle for political power in 2016, pollster's impact on the election, historical relationships and candidates' campaign rhetoric, post-election events that occurred after the election and the effect on one's psychic. It also highlights the impact of nationalism, white supremacy, and the Alt-right movement and leftist groups. It attempts to give clarity to an event such as Charlottesville, Virginia in 2017 and why it happened. This book is an excellent source for checking one beliefs system when it comes to human rights and equal rights under the laws.

This book will help support classroom teachers and students (based on their age group and education levels) by providing valuable information to supplement the curriculum as well as the broader community. Our goal was to promote an understanding of the role the news media, technology, and how social networking impacted daily events in the Whitehouse and United States Congress during the 2016 presidential campaign during and after the election. This book also included the impact of the assimilation of misinformation, extreme controversy, reality television formats, lies, political scandals, social media and cyber warfare as instruments used to influence the election results.

As educators, we have dedicated 63 years of our lives to teaching and learning. We hope, this book is a profound, challenging, exciting, and a useful, compelling educational tool and read for ordinary people in the United States and the global community. Why, because "Knowledge is Power."

Glossary

"Facebook, Twitter, YouTube, Instagram, and Trolling Definitions"

(1) ***Facebook*** is an American for-profit corporation and an online social media and social networking service based in Menlo Park, California.

(2) ***Tweeter*** is a social networking website, which allows users to publish short messages that are visible to other users. These messages are known as tweets, and can only be 140 characters or less in length.

(3) ***YouTube*** is a video sharing service that allows users to watch videos posted by other users and upload videos of their own. The service was started as an independent website in 2005 and was acquired by Google in 2006.

(4) ***Instagram*** is a social networking app made for sharing photos and videos from a smartphone. Similar to Facebook or Twitter, everyone who creates an Instagram account has a profile and a news-feed. When you post a photo or video on Instagram, it will be displayed on your profile.

(5) ***Troll or Trolling:*** A person who sows discord on the ***Internet*** by starting quarrels or upsetting people, by posting inflammatory, extraneous, or off-topic messages in an online community (such as a newsgroup, forum, chat room, or blog) with the intent of provoking readers into an emotional frenzy.

References

Department of Justice. (n.d). [APA]). Retrieved from https://www.justice.gov/

Hulse, C. (2017).Trump Fences himself in with border wall spending threat". Retrieved from: https://www.nytimes.com/2017/08/24/us/politics/trump-wall- government- shutdown-congress.html

Homophobic. Retrieved from http://www.idsnews.com. Title: Column: Donald Trump promote a racist, sexist, and homophobic agenda. Wenninger, E. (2015). Homophobic.

Donald Trump Promotes a Racist, Sexist, and Homophobic Agenda. Retrieved from http://www.idsnews.com.

Enzernik, S. (2017). Asiatic Barred Zone - The 1917 Immigration Act that presaged

Trumps' Travel Ban. Retrieved from www. https://daily.jstor.org/?s=Asiatic+barred+Zone

Department of Justice. (n.d). [APA], (n.d.). Retrieved from https://www.justice.gov/

Farley, R. (2017). No Evidence Sanctuary Cities 'Breed Crime'. Retrieved from http://www.factcheck.org/

Berger, J.M. (2016). How the White Nationalists Learned to Love Donald Trump Retrieved from http://www.politico.com/magazine/story/2016/10/donald-trump- 2016- white-nationalists-alt-right-214388

Urban Christian News. (2017). Why Many Conservatives Have Lined up Behind Trump. (2017). Retrieved from http://www.urbanchristiannews.com

Tyson, A., & Maniam, S. (2016). Behind Trumps' Victory: Divisions by Race, Gender and Education. Pew Research Center Retrieved from http:// www.perresearch.org

Obeldallah, D. (2017). Why Putin and Trump both like Marine Le Pen. Retrieved from www.cnn.com

Olsen, H. (2016). Can the Republican Party Keep Trump Dems? National Review. Retrieved from http://www.nationalreview.com

Kailan, Herb, Diaz, 2017). Trump signs bill approving new sanctions against Russia. Retrieved from www.cnn.com

Drum, K. (2016). Mother Jones: Is Steve Bannon Racist? Let's Find Out! Retrieved from www.motherjones.com

Honocki, E. (2017). Media Matters- Breibart Reporter Is a White Nationalist With a Long Trail of Racist and Anti-Muslim Twitter. Retrieved from https://www.mediamatters.org/

Nguygen, T. (2017). Steve Bannon is leaving the White House. Retrieved from www.vanityfair.com/news: by Tina Nguyen- 8/18/17

Ehrenfreud, M. (2017). What it means for the rich, the world and for you. Retrieved from https://www.washington post.com.

Somin, I. (2017). Trump's order on Sanctuary Cities is Dangerous and unconstitutional. Retrieved from www.learnliberty.org

MSNBC (2017).Few Republicans Defend Trump After Comey Hearing June 9, 2017. Retrieved from www.msnbc.com

Farenthold & O'Connell, 2017). Washington Post: Democracy Dies in darkness by David A. Farenthold and Jonathan O'Connell. Retrieved from https://www.washingtonpost.com

Rowe vs. Wade. (1973). Retrieved from http://caselaw.find/law.com/us-supreme- court/410/113.html

Planned Parenthood. (2017). Retrieved from: https:// www.plannedparenthood.org

Beckwith & Alter. (2017). Draining the Swamp. Retrieved from www.http://www.time.com/donald-trump-drain-swamp/

News Media Networks and Print Media in Support of Trump (2017). Retrieved from: http://nymag.com:

Trumps Cabinet Appointments (2017). Retrieved from www.mcclatchydc.com/news/politics-government.

Cohen, C. (2017). Donald Trump Sexism Tracker: Every Offensive Comment in one Place. The Telegraph Lifestyle/Women www.telegraph.co.uk/woman/politics

Sexism [Def 1]. (n.d.). Vocabulary.com dictionary. Retrieved from https://www.vocabularycom/dictionary/sexism

Huffington Post. (June, 5, 2013). Latino Voices. Retrieved from http:/www.huffingtonpost.com

Sebastian, M. (2017). Trump's Campaign Manager, Kelly Ann Conway. Retrieved from http://www.cosmopolitan.com/politics

Electoral College. (2017). Retrieved from http://www.history.com/topics/electoral-college

Ball, M. (2016). Donald Trump and the Politics of Fear. Retrieved from Atlantic Magazine. www.theatlantic.com

Southern Poverty Law Center. (n.d.). Alternative Right. Retrieved from https://www.splcenter.org/fighting-hate/extremist-files/ideology/alternative-right

DACA. (n.d.). Deferred Action for Childhood Arrivals. Retrieved from https://en.wikipedia.org/wiki/Deferred_Action_for_Childhood_Arrivals

Emoluments Clause [Def 2]. (n.d.). Retrieved from https:// www.bing.com

Obstruction of Justice [Def 3]. (n.d.). Retrieved from www.cnn.com

Appiah, A. (2014). Extrinsic and Intrinsic Racism and Cultural Racisms. University of Minnesota Press.

Anderson, Claude. (2015). Dr. Claude Anderson explains the definition of racism.v=Qi9imppcCUc. Retrieved from https://www.youtube.com/watch?

News Media Networks and Print Media in Support of Trump (2017). Retrieved from http://nymag.com:

Davenport, Kelsey, (n.d.) Chronology of U.S.-North Korean Nuclear and Missile https://www.armscontrol.og/factsheets/dprkchron

Rosen, D. (n.d.). Illegal Drugs, Race and the 2016 Elections-Counterpunch. http://www.counterpunch.org/2016/03/18/illegal-drugs-race-and-the-2018-elections/

Election results based on race, gender, age, education and class/graphical data source. http://www.pewresearch.center.org/2016/09/14/ http://factcheck.org

Electoral Votes vs Popular/statistical data source/https://www.whitehouse.gov/the-press-office/2017/11/27/wall-street-journal-tax-reform-growth-and-deficit

https://www.whitehouse.gov/briefing-room/presidential-actions:

https://www.whitehouse.gov/briefing-room/signed-legislation?field_legislation_status_value=0&page=1

Printed in the United States
By Bookmasters